About the book

Innovation and transformation are risky, even terrifying, concepts, but not more terrifying than what happens to the 56 million students in the U.S. whose futures depend on us if we don't do something *today*. If we believe we cannot fail the next generation, then the systemic reform of American public education is a national imperative!

In her book, Trina shares why.....

- Maintaining failing structures — both ideological and physical — and tinkering with existing systems won't generate the results that are necessary.

- It is not enough to create new models, no matter how interesting, engaging, or philosophically on track they may be. The problem with incorporating the great new models of learning into our educational system is exactly that: *we are incorporating them into our educational system.*

- Technology is a tool, not the answer to improving the education system, and it means nothing without the right people, processes, training and support behind the implementation.

- There is an entire subculture of online activity, networking, and authentic experiences that is creating another whole

i

dimension for digital learners; and understanding how these learners rely on their technology is a necessary component to educating them.

- The new role of the educational union must be to take an active and aggressive stand in laying the framework for a new era that will lead to the rebirth of the American Education System as a system that meets the needs of both the 21st century learner and the 21st century teacher.

- Our education system must be restructured to teach learners how to navigate the information overload that surrounds them every day.

- We must begin to teach children *how* to learn, rather than *what* to learn, and from that, how to apply the knowledge gained.

- We must encourage and support school leadership in this new environment and create a climate where innovation is not stamped out before it even begins because school leaders are afraid to fail.

Contents

Acknowledgments

It would be impossible for me to list all of the people who have made a difference in the world of education and from whom I draw personal inspiration. I am surrounded on a daily basis by people who are so committed to the mission and vision of educating children. I could go back, much like a timeline of my personal growth and identify people who have inspired me, educated me, pushed and encouraged me onto new levels in much the same way each of you reading this book remember a favorite teacher from elementary school or from college. There are also those who gave me my first job as a rookie teacher fresh "off the boat" from Ireland, and those who mentored and coached me for decades. You know who you are, and I thank each and every one of you for the contribution you made in my journey thus far.

As everyone who's ever written anything knows, there are a few people who make it their personal mission to force you to actually finish the project once it has started and it is that small team of "nagging" colleagues and family that I'd like to thank here.

Steve Miller, Brad Lineberger, Victoria Pylvainen, Ivan Cohen, Angelina O'Brien, Eric Allen, Kathy Schaaf, Rick Angelone, and Landy Tiffany provided me with support, research assistance, editing, and plain old-fashioned pushing to get the job done! I appreciate each and every one of you, and value your continued commitment to creating awareness of the need for access to high-quality education for all learners.

A special thanks to my husband Luis and to my beautiful daughters Allison and Courtney for putting up with my late night computer activity! Your support has encouraged me, and my hope is that you girls will know you can do anything you aspire to do if you make an effort.

Foreword

A short while ago, I received a call from Trina Angelone asking whether I would be willing to write a foreword to her new publication. I informed her I would prefer reading it first, and a few days later, a draft of the book was on my desk. I had other work, but I could not put her book down. Her preface caught my interest, and when I completed the introduction, I knew that it would be an honor to write the foreword.

This publication should be read by every teacher, teacher-to-be, every principal and every parent. Business leaders, politicians, clergy and others should read this as well. I certainly reinforce her request for all those who have responsibility for public education. When you read Trina's words, think about how we can incorporate her ideas and suggestions to transform public education so that students are ready to participate in the technology age of the 21st century.

It is a transformation based on preparing students to advocate for and utilize the technology age—to actually become a player in the 21st century implementing a curriculum where technology is seen as a "tool", where students have time to explore the past and dream about the future—THEIR FUTURE. The school is not just a building, but through technology, a total learning environment. Therefore, with the use of smart phones, iPads, and the "Library of Congress", they can teach themselves (given the two cultural imperatives of English and Math). Each student then becomes the class. Each deserves the time to acquire the skills and methodology necessary to become independent self-learners. All of the above is just part of what the author is advocating.

Transformation is not easy. It takes a community who believe in educating all children for a future which is uncertain and ever-changing. They must believe in a culture which believes in the future and a dream that we can all be players in the 21st century.

Talk about bringing a dream into reality.

The man who inspired Trina also served on the Board of Nova Southeastern University, (NSU). This university was started fifty years ago by a small group of men with a vision and a dream. Wayne Huizenga joined with them later and helped to bring that dream into reality, especially the Business School which bears his name. NSU is now a university providing education from "birth" through "elder age".

Another dream which became a reality.

Stressed throughout the book is the argument that it will not be enough to give students a piece of equipment; a smart phone, an iPad, etc... unless the climate of utilization of these tools provides the feedback to move from the building "into the world". These tools enable self-learners to communicate with others anywhere in the world, to speak to experts from many different countries, and not be restricted to the text book. We want to promote self-learners and motivate them to explore areas in which they are interested through the use of world communications. Rather than restrict the use of any of the above tools, we should encourage their use so that students can explore their interests and move into true inquiry.

I want to thank Trina for writing this stimulating and readable book about a positive transformation in our schools today. Hopefully it will encourage others to join with her to move public education forward.

Abraham S. Fischler
President Emeritus/University Professor
Nova Southeastern University

Preface
Who am I to write
this book?

I am an educator, a 30 year veteran at that, but this is not a grand educational piece of work. I am also a business woman who has had the extraordinary good fortune to have met some outstanding educators and entrepreneurs along the way. This book is not written primarily for educators and certainly does not contain a lot of educational acronyms or other industry based terminology. Consider this more of a conversation, a public service announcement that encourages people to take a fresh look at the American public school system and everything that will be necessary in the coming years to solve the problems we're facing.

Why did I write this book now? It's easy... A colleague, Tom Vander Ark, signed a copy of his book to me with the following words "Thanks for helping America and the world Get Smart!" and I realized immediately that I actually wasn't doing anything to increase public awareness regarding the need to support our public school system during the period of transformation into a technological age. With so much focus on creating alternatives to the public school system, so much bashing of public schools and educators in the media, it seemed an appropriate time for someone to step up and say that this is not the way to solve our problems, that decades of tinkering with the existing system or creating new models that still reside within the existing system of education as we know it, will have no long term impact. Significant change requires significant systemic reform and will require public support. It is very clear that "school choice" is quickly becoming the mainstream norm, and as such, we must ensure that those who chose public school, or those without options to choose anything else, receive the highest quality, world-class education in those public schools.

I consider myself very fortunate to have been able to experience phenomenal opportunities that the United States has to offer. I have lived the American dream insomuch as I am an immigrant from Ireland, one who arrived in this country because her father's restaurant was bombed during "the troubles" in the late 1970's in Belfast, Northern Ireland. I don't believe that as a teacher in Ireland I would have been able to experience the rich and full career I have had as a direct result of being in the United States. I have taught in high schools both public and private, I've been an administrator at both public and private K-12 programs, have served as the principal for a university virtual school, have owned my own private school, and even crossed over to the "dark side" and had a career in the corporate world as an educational vendor. I share all of this not because it is important for you to know that I have experiences in both education and in business, but because it is important and for you to know that there are thousands of people just like me who are working in America's schools. They are hard-working individuals, people who have great ideas, people who are open to the great ideas of others, and people who really need to have a voice in the transformation of public education.

About five years ago, I met a man, a very ordinary looking man... And while he came from humble roots, he was more than the sum of his childhood experiences and poor beginnings. This "extra ordinary" man had led an even more extraordinary life. Meeting Wayne Huizenga (think

Blockbuster, Marlins, Waste Management, etc.,) was a transformational moment in my life, and while that sounds like I "drank the Kool-Aid" and found this business tycoon inspirational, make no mistake, while I was in awe of the great things he had done, I was much more impressed by the commitment he made to give me an opportunity to make a difference. He did indeed invest in my vision, and although I am no longer personally involved with that company, Wayne inspired something more important and long-lasting for me as an individual, and that was in the words we shook the deal on, "Dream it, dream big, then do it ten times bigger than that, and above all... just make sure it works!"

It is on those words from Wayne Huizenga that I reflect when I say we need to transform American education. Every child in our school classrooms today deserves an opportunity to be taught by a master teacher, to use world-class curriculum, to interact with engaging and exciting new technologies, to experience collaborating with students outside their local neighborhood, and to be exposed to cultures and languages other than their own, in order to prepare them for opportunities in the global economy. It is only when we get "education" right that America's children will be able to dream big...

If we believe we cannot fail the next generation, then the systemic reform of American public education is a national imperative!

http://SystemicReform.com

Rescuing the American Education System from The System

1 Why Johnny *still* can't read

It's tempting to describe the American educational system as being at a crossroads; one where, if we choose the right path, we can fulfill our obligations to students and to society as a whole by providing an education that prepares this generation of young people to enter the 21st century economy. But the truth is that we've already reached that crossroads more than once, and time and time again we've decided to stay on the familiar path. As a result, we're falling further and further behind.

This isn't news.

We've been aware of the problem for more than a generation.

In 1983, *A Nation at Risk: The Imperative for Educational Reform* set off shockwaves with its critique of the various ways American students had been declining in achievement since the early 1960s, though hardly any of its recommendations were implemented. The school year, in light of the *Nation at Risk* report, remains too short, as does the school day. Compensation for teachers stands largely immune from market forces, and standardized testing of students and teachers alike remains an inadequate measure of achievement and talent.

And even as the report's findings were ignored, the concerns that motivated it in the first place have taken us in the wrong direction. That well-intentioned focus on crafting national, standardized metrics for measuring student achievement has led to an expansion of the industrial age "factory model" of education, focused on testing based on standards that are formed by committee, and whose results have little relevance to the 21st century workplace our students are graduating into.

Even as tests change, standards change, and policies change, in essence the implementation of education as a model — as a process of teaching and learning — stays stagnant.

Even the most reluctant-to-change-anything educator would have a hard time saying that the way things are going is working for anyone. Less than 33% of eighth graders are proficient in math and over 75% of students graduating high school can't master algebra, a staggering statistic that rears its ugly head when we correlate that to the percentage of students entering college who find themselves in remedial or pre-college algebra classes. This is even more shocking when we consider that annual spending on education stands at $15,171 per student, nationwide, according to a recent study by The Organization for Economic Cooperation and Development.

Meanwhile, proponents of change suggest that the answers lie in even more spending, more technology in the schools, and a better teacher-to-student ratio. While it's possible that these would lead to some incremental improvements in test scores, they still do not address the root of the problem, a reality that says we need more than superficial patches.

2

A glossy coat of paint doesn't address the need for structural reinvention.

The factory model treats all students as identical cogs in a machine. It's not personalized, and it doesn't evolve to fit the rapidly changing world our children will inherit from us.

While I was personally offended with the "factory floor" analogy coined in recent years, knowing that there are many exceptional things going on in our schools, the reality is that, in many ways, schools *are* reminiscent of a factory. **However, the significant difference is that education is a business that produces a product that's incredibly hard to quantify, which is why it's so hard to determine how to improve the assembly line. That product is human cognition.**

In any other manufacturing industry or factory, the workers have a specific design for building the model, based upon a prototype and data gathered from piloting or beta testing. While there can be differences in raw materials, differences in the assembly line tools, and human interventions, at the end of the day the product is clearly defined, made up of clearly established materials, and is built according to a roadmap that clearly identifies the desired outcome. Any deviations are relatively easy to track, and it's actually easy to see where errors occurred if the final product does not meet the specifications, is not built according to a certain timeline, or if the results are simply unacceptable.

In the case of education, it's a lot more complex. There are way too many variables. In fact, every human being is unique, and every learner comes into the educational environment with widely varying backgrounds, exposure to language, socioeconomic status, philosophical differences, and many more reference points. With so much variation in those raw materials at one end of the assembly line, it's no surprise that the factory model falls apart by the time we get to the finished product. To push the analogy further, add to this mix the fact that the assembly line workers are often very inexperienced, the tools they're given to work with are outdated, factory budgets are strained, and even the blueprints, design and roadmaps that they're given to work with vary from factory to factory, it becomes virtually impossible to guarantee that any students coming out of this process will actually end up looking like the same model of anything when they graduate.

While the world has changed dramatically in the thirty years since *A Nation at Risk*, our schools have not. And that failure to adapt affects us all in fundamental ways, even if we're those lucky few whose children are in schools that manage to meet most of their needs.

A thriving public school system is necessary to preserve quality of life in our communities. In fact, I'd argue that the role of the school in *creating* and *maintaining* a sense of community is more important than ever. As technology leads more and more of us to live in exclusively virtual worlds, and our work days grow longer because we can always be reached by email or social media, the shared physical spaces of public schools remain vital touchstones of common experience and a cornerstone of any neighborhood.

To preserve the quality of American life, and ensure that our democracy functions in a way that reflects the values and ideals of our citizens, we have to

find a way to restore the educational system of our country to its past glory, while not necessarily having it look like the same model. The way to do that is not by focusing on, literally, "old-school" approaches — the teaching of "Reading, Writing and Arithmetic" as it were — but rather in implementing new ways to engage students and empower educators.

Along the way, we have to reevaluate every piece of the system, and redefine necessary essential building blocks in the teaching and learning process. How do we define "successful"? How critical is educational experience if the experience was gained in a system we find less than adequate? Do we test for pure knowledge of facts, or do we adjust for the complexity of the knowledge gained? Are we trying to evaluate a student's character and (to use a sadly out-of-favor phrase) citizenship? And how do we judge if a student is prepared to join the workforce in tomorrow's global economy?

Every time the technology that enables today's children to have better access to information than any teacher can provide becomes more commonly available, our schools grow less and less relevant to their students. And to put that in perspective, a student today has access to more information via the Internet in a single day than their grandparents had access to in their entire lifetime. It really makes us question what education today should be about because we know one thing for sure, it certainly cannot be about learning facts about who, what, where, or when, because that information — in other words everything that we have in our textbooks — is readily available at our fingertips.

5

The much bigger question is, can our education system be restructured to teach learners how to navigate the information overload that surrounds them every day? Can we begin to teach children *how* to learn, rather than *what* to learn, and from that, how to apply the knowledge gained?

Teaching these complex, higher-order skills of critical thinking at an earlier point in the educational process than is typically done is a vital step to reforming what we teach today's students, and it's something that cannot be taught using a textbook or even an e-text. It's a change that will most definitely require a whole new set of teaching standards, new evaluation standards, and indeed a complete shakeup of education as we know it.

What's necessary is more than just reform. What's needed is a revolutionary, ground-up approach to reinventing every aspect of the educational system.

2 What are we training kids towards?

Traditionally, we've looked at the purpose of public education as equipping students to go to a university or college or else directly into the workforce. The junior-college system was designed to provide those students who were otherwise left out with access to vocational training for manufacturing and blue-collar jobs.

As we have seen in many towns in the Northeast, when industrial or manufacturing jobs disappear, the school system designed to provide those businesses with workers is put in an impossible spot, as declining industry inevitably leads to failing learners being the only ones trying to find those jobs. Much as the students are falling behind as technology changes, the community college and junior-college system previously designed to support the manufacturing and vocational industry is in great danger of falling behind as well.

The challenge facing that system is how to retain a role of influence and value, not by becoming another college or university offering degree programs (as seems to be the current trend), but by striving to provide the foundation for retraining learners in a new age, one

7

where the concept of staying in a job for 30 to 40 years is extinct.

Today's workers can expect to change jobs at least five to seven times during their lifetime, and many will require lifelong education and reeducation in order to support complete career changes. The average worker today stays at a job for 4.4 years, according to the most recent available data from the Bureau of Labor Statistics, but the expected tenure of the workforce's youngest employees is about half that.

Ninety-one percent of Millennials (born between 1977-1997) expect to stay in a job for less than three years, according to the Future Workplace "Multiple Generations @ Work" survey, resulting in a likely scenario of having 15 – 20 jobs over the course of their working lives.

Our nation will rely upon the community college system and programs such as those workforce development agencies provide to help our workforce remain current, viable employees in a global economy. One of the biggest problems facing us today is the fact that these agencies, much like K-12, still function exactly as they have for the past couple of decades. A massive overhaul is an essential in the community college system if it is to remain viable or relevant as the cornerstone for training and retraining our adult workforce.

The University model hasn't changed either, and also fails to produce graduates with the skills necessary to get the jobs that need to be filled in the modern economy. Actually, the problem here is ten times greater than the problem in the

K-12 space. In these "hallowed halls," not much has changed in 100 years.

Yes, there are pockets of great innovation, and many good things going on in our community college and university systems, but the reality is that tenure, jurisdictional boundaries, and teacher work schedules that require 12 to 15 hours of work per week — surrounded by office hours and research time — have promoted a culture with zero pressure to produce any tangible or concrete results. While there are internal accountability standards and accreditation measures, the bottom line is that, because people pay privately or use scholarship dollars to attend college, there is no real public scrutiny regarding the job performance of those colleges.

Again, I have no doubt that there are great things going on in many of our colleges, and valuable research that will make a difference in many of our lives. However, there is nothing like public accountability, or the capacity for a state college to act like a private school in an entrepreneurial manner — crossing jurisdictional or state boundaries in a competitive spirit, complete with competitive pricing and programs, competitive salaries and opportunities — to begin to change process at the higher education level. Don't get me wrong, there is absolutely a place for the university experience, those lazy days with a couple of classes, the professor with a classical-education background, the science labs, the whole social experience of sororities, frat houses and football games, but, at some point, it has to realign and refocus to become relevant to today's world.

At every level, as technological innovation happens *outside* the classroom with increasing speed, it's impossible for any of these moribund institutional models to keep up and give graduates what they need to perform effectively. From outdated trade schools to an unchanged university model, students are graduating without the skills necessary to qualify for the jobs that the modern economy needs to have filled.

The full spectrum of education, from kindergarten through college, must be reconsidered. The model needs to be rebuilt.

In their book *Disrupting Class: How Disruptive Innovation Will Change the Way the World Learns* (McGraw-Hill, 2008), authors Clayton Christensen, Curtis W. Johnson, and Michael B. Horn apply Christensen's "disruption" approach to education in much the way he approached business in his best-selling *The Innovator's Dilemma* a few years earlier. However, while the work does a good job at drawing attention to the things that need to change, offering the model of "blended learning" in all its forms or adaptations as a way to update the classroom experience in the digital age, it falls short of offering a path that will actually achieve transformative change.

Disruption is, at its core, an awareness or acknowledgment that something is not working and that we need to abandon the old way of approaching a situation to focus on new models. But that awareness, in and of itself, does not lead to systemic reform.

Christensen, Johnson, and Horn identify a number of new models, including what is today commonly referred to as "blended learning," in which technology is infused into the classroom and we play with schedules, labs, and different technologies in an effort to create a flexible, individualized, customized learning process.

There's little doubt that technology needs to play a significant role if we are to have a truly modern educational system. At the root of the problem of why schools are not producing graduates with tech-based "soft skills" that businesses demand is the way K-12 deploys technology instruction, which is generally insufficient, sporadic, and often done without adequate preparation across the system.

In the long term, the stakes are high. Access to, and understanding of, technology is a key factor in bridging the gap between rich and poor throughout the world. But while disrupting education and, along with it, finding lower-cost ways of putting modern technology into the hands of teachers and students, is a necessary goal, I maintain that disrupting education is merely step one.

A much deeper problem exists at the core of American education, one that requires a much more complex solution.

It is not enough to create new models, no matter how interesting, engaging, or philosophically on track they may be. Even if we are getting promising results through the implementation of these new models in small pockets of high-quality instruction or in particularly innovative school districts around the country, the problem with incorporating the great new models of blended learning into our educational system is exactly that: *we are incorporating them into our educational system.*

If we take these innovations, new theories that incorporate an understanding of how children learn in our digital age, great new concepts and practices for personalizing the educational process, and tremendous advancements in the world of technology, and put all of them into the same educational system that has already been falling short, they will quickly be smothered in archaic systems throughout the country and soon after be written off as failures. Good ideas will be rejected because the implementation was inadequate, and another generation will be left behind while we search in vain for the next big idea.

The only way *all* children will have the opportunity to engage in a high quality 21ˢᵗ century education that will set them apart from the students that came before them — one that fully prepares them to engage in the global economy — is if we acknowledge that large-scale systemic reform must take place within *all* of the systems that make up the grand educational system itself.

I understand that this is tantamount to calling for a revolution, saying we must create an entirely new way of designing, implementing, and governing, with a whole new set of rules, policies, regulations, laws, standards, budgets, expectations, deliverables, and so on, in essence, a redesign of what we consider to be the American Educational System.

In 2011, "A Futuristic Vision for 21ˢᵗ Century Education" (*ASCD Express*, Vol. 6, No. 11, © 2011, ASCD) argued that, in order to build a personal learning network (PLN), "We need to be visionary. We are not marching slowly into the future; we are speeding toward it in a whirlwind frenzy, mandated by exponential rate of change. As educators we must continuously ask ourselves, what do students need to learn to succeed in the world to come? A world we can't even imagine."

I propose *we need an educational revolution that is planned, strategic, and executed with a dedicated commitment to the mission and vision of transforming American education.*

3   Clothing can be vintage, schools cannot

There are many criticisms and even more critics of the American education system, from politicians who believe that mandating excellence is the way to go, to every person who's ever attended school and feels that they could do a better job because things happening in American schools today never happened when *they* attended.

But the reality is that every generation, upon reaching adulthood, looks back with the proverbial rose-tinted glasses and imagines that their school experience was so much superior to the one the students are receiving today, while in actuality it's more like my grandparents thinking that my mother's rock 'n roll generation were the kids from hell while my mother thought that the punk-rock music that I grew up on was beyond anything she would consider appropriate for young ears (wonder what any of them would say about today's rap and hip-hop).

Other fields, such as medicine and the law, are a big part of daily life, but the criticisms people offer of those areas are far more benign — or at least much more specific — than the more general, scattershot attacks on education. For instance, while people wax nostalgic for the days when doctors made house calls, few would argue that doctors aren't better than ever at diagnosing disorders or that prescribed treatments haven't become more effective at treating them.

So why does the world at large find so much "back in my day…" style fault in education but not offer that same sort of ad hominem criticism of other fields?

It's because we have allowed the profession of education and the business of educating children to become stagnant for nearly a century.

Almost as soon as American mass education began, it began to ossify, freezing in place. While all other aspects of modern culture and society have gone through transformations based upon the technologies which have become part of those particular segments of our society — how many stores do you go to that don't have a bar-code reader at checkout? — education remains the only field in which someone traveling in time from a hundred years ago could come back and not only recognize a classroom as a familiar place (though they'd be confused by the fashions), but step right back into their own job as the teacher.

Each generation infuses the technology of the day into the classroom, but while the covers on the textbooks may look prettier, and the pictures are certainly of higher quality, at the end of the day the teacher who was at the front of the classroom a century ago as the grand purveyor of knowledge still essentially functions in that capacity in many classrooms across the United States. And the student who may have written on a slate or on paper, taking down notes, reading aloud, and completing worksheets, is still essentially performing the same tasks in the same manner, even if they're using a laptop or tablet computer.

Oh, we have had many great ideas come and almost as many go, we have had old math and "new math." We've tried to "think metric." We moved away from the one-room schoolhouse and Abe Lincoln doing his homework in coal on the back of a shovel (even lined loose leaf paper was a technological innovation once) to individual classrooms divided by grade level and subject area; and quills being supplanted by ballpoint pens.

We eventually rolled back around to open-concept spaces with multi-subject and multi-grade-level groupings to reflect the changing needs of schools and students.

We have had chalkboards, green boards, whiteboards, and many more grand inventions and even grander programs cross our educational doorways. We have had great legislation (not enough) and poor legislation (far, far too much); funded and unfunded mandates; we have tested children in every direction until both the children and the teachers have arrived at a stage where each new "idea" is greeted with an understanding that "this too shall pass."

And the classroom door closes and the teacher stands at the front of the room working with 25 or 30 students who still reluctantly take notes, and classroom life goes on with only the most superficial changes.

So what on earth is wrong with this barely changed picture? I'd say that half the teachers in the country would probably answer that absolutely nothing needs to be changed, and if your child is fortunate enough to be in the classroom with an outstanding educator, you'd probably agree that it's okay to leave well enough alone.

16

But this isn't about what you want, it isn't about what I want, and it isn't about what the teacher likes or doesn't like, it's about how students learn in this new digital age, and how the profession of education should be transforming to focus on a teaching and learning process suited to this new age.

The best change of the first century of mass education is that all children — regardless of class, race, or gender — have access to public education. The impact of this cannot be understated as a shift that truly reshaped America and reflected the purest ideals of our democracy.

But now that universal access to public education is a given, what is the goal? Surely it cannot simply be access to education, or the across-the-board achievement of a minimum set of standards we can test with state-mandated assessments?

In our efforts to educate all children, to provide equity of access to a free public education, we have managed to really limit what we are providing access to; it's almost as though we've codified underachievement by aiming at the lowest common denominator. Doing the minimum possible for the greatest number of students doesn't do anybody any favors. As a result, people really do feel like they've won the lottery when their child receives a voucher to attend private school or is selected to attend a charter school. As a lifelong public educator, it's embarrassing to be able to say that Americans are excited and grateful to be able to escape from the public education system.

The system is failing students and society at large by producing graduates incapable of finding jobs and growing the economy. Unemployed graduates don't generate the tax revenues that provide schools for the next generation of students, and things get worse.

The system is failing our educators too, failing to empower them to make a difference.

So how do we *solve* the problem?

4 Solving for how (not *why*)

For the past hundred years, learning has been a largely passive process. Students are expected to absorb lessons, do largely rote memorization exercises, and then graduate when they can accurately regurgitate the information on exams (okay, I'll admit this may be a little unfair, but it's part of why many adults can't remember much of what they learned in school - memorization is not comprehension). The digital era, where students engage the web for answers to every question easily dozens of times a day, demands a different approach.

There are many innovative and creative things going on in public education today and there are many states beginning to identify the need for systemic reform. Our goal should be to create a non-passive, more-active model for education. We need to take the pieces we like from a variety of approaches — there is no "one size fits all" solution — mix and match to redesign the teaching and learning process. In the 2Revolution models (www.2revolutions.net), Adam Rubin, Bryan Setser, and Todd kern call this a "learning integrated by design" approach to reforming the system from the inside out.

Their model requires that kids are involved and willing to work. But the beauty of what we're talking about here is that, in success, students will be more engaged than they've ever been before. With the freedom to use the technology that is already a part of their daily lives outside of schools, education will seem less like a forced task and more like, well, not play, but more like a hobby they're passionate about.

What does this really mean?

In reality it means that we're training students to be lifelong learners, which will be vital when they enter a constantly changing workforce and need to acquire new skills to be able to keep up, advance, or change careers.

Learning, using the knowledge, and teaching others... this may sound familiar, and in fact it is.

Kids learn better when they have an opportunity to practice what they've learned and then teach it to someone else. In the days of the one-room schoolhouse, teachers would use the older kids who could already read to help teach the younger ones. Born of necessity, it was a technique that helped reinforce the lessons for those older kids even as it enlarged the circle of knowledge. Even as adults, how many of us remember something much better when we actually have to demonstrate how to do it to someone else, or share what we did with another person?

We already know that to hear or to see new information is step one, but to interact with that new material, and to reuse it either by teaching others or doing something with it, is how we will move from lower- to higher-order cognition. It is a practice employed by educators at the elementary and secondary levels, and is used by every institution from medical schools to trade schools.

20

It's just common sense, and it's something we already know about how human beings process and learn in general. What makes the 2Revolutions model interesting is that the approach applies the principles of universal design for learning in a technology-based approach to blended learning for today's digital students. In action, an example of making the kids the relevant focal point of learning may be seen in my own virtual school, where teachers are expected to host live, interactive whiteboard sessions once a week. In these sessions, students share what they have learned, demonstrating, teaching, and creating a community around the learning process. This provides a more meaningful online experience than merely a social one. Students archive samples of their best work, and teachers are invited to share in collaborative groups within the individual student's virtual portfolio, an invitation that comes from the student who owns the portfolio experience. That's not to say that there isn't a time and place for social interaction in an online environment, but that's another chapter!

In the modern classroom, the idea of collaborative sessions with peers where, once a week, students would have to teach what they learned to others hearkens back to not just the one-room schoolhouse model, but even further back to how masters taught apprentices in the days when there was no widely available schooling outside of the home. We don't have to go back too many generations to recognize that system, the one that was replaced by the community college system, the trade schools, and the business schools.

I am not, however, suggesting that reforming education today is simply a matter of redesigning how we do lesson plans or some other tweaks within the classroom as we know it. It has to be more than that, because more of the same won't change anything, and ongoing tweaking and course-correcting adjustments being made to the existing system will probably never get us to a true transformation. We have to consider education as an entire spectrum, a complex system of complex sub-systems.

There are those who would argue that the latest thing in education today is mass virtual education and that virtual education is the way to reform the system as we know it.

This thought has put fear into the hearts of teachers and educational support staff as they listen to politicians and others extol the demise of "teaching as we know it" and the impending mass reduction of the educational workforce. The same concept has come surrounded with stories of how it will significantly reduce our expenditure in education as we will be able to educate hundreds of thousands of students in MOOCs (massively open online courses) with a single teacher, without much thought for the infrastructure, policies, processes, and transactions that need to occur in a world migrating from bricks and mortar to online on any grand scale.

Virtual education is not going away, nor should it, but virtual education in itself is not the answer to the need for reform initiatives. Virtual education's significant role and increasing importance is certainly an indicator that something new is past due.

But while the idea of virtual schooling is no longer a fringe learning modality (adults of every age use it to self-teach, as the literally millions of YouTube videos on everything from how to tie a bowtie to performing CPR readily attest), our goal must be to find something truly new in the way we blend different kinds of learning while integrating flexibility of choices into the mix at all levels.

There will come a day, and it's not in the distant future, when education will become a full-choice model. This model will allow the parent to be allocated X dollars per student, and that parent and student will be allowed to shop for the best quality and variety of services from a wide range of providers – public, private, and corporate – to match their educational needs as identified on an individualized education plan.

The providers will be selected by students and parents as part of a school choice continuum of services designed not according to the Carnegie unit, but rather mapped to a set of standards and competencies which need to be mastered prior to moving on to the next level.

The depth and breadth of learning along this continuum for each individual child will be based upon the child's starting point, interests, talents, goals and aspirations, and so too will the family's ability to select from a wide variety of choices when determining who provides the education for their child and when.

For reform to work, we need to be clear about our expectations and our willingness to accept a new model for how we do pretty much everything related to the education process.

Letting go of beliefs that have been inculcated for over a hundred years is just the beginning. At every level of government — federal, local, and state — we have to embrace a new approach.

Key to this process is letting go of anything punitive. Far too often in recent years, anything truly new being put into the schools is constrained by so many different rules and restrictions — some born out of genuine concern about students' well-being, others driven far more often by fears of controversy and lawsuits — that any chance of innovation is crushed under the weight.

We absolutely cannot create an environment of reform if it has to function from a place of fear, and all too often education provides the grand distraction in the political arena that steers public opinion towards bashing our educational system as an easy target.

5   Rewards are worth the risk

The risks we most associate with young people using computers in classrooms today tend to revolve around social media — Instagram, Facebook, text messaging, to name a few examples — and how this social media can lead to cyber bullying and online harassment. High-profile incidents involving sending, receiving, or forwarding sexually explicit messages, photographs, or images via cell phone, computer, or other digital devices also known as "sexting" have parents understandably worried about their children, and schools similarly worried about their students and about how to discourage this behavior. I can remember an incident in early 2000 during my tenure as principal of a very large brick and mortar public high school, when some students created a video with inappropriate content at home, inserted shots they had cleverly taken during the school day, and then made their video public online much to the shame of about a dozen students.

Since this was over a decade ago, when such things were far less common than they are today, the incident sparked the interest of the mass media and resulted in multiple suspensions and recommendations for expulsion based on what I believed in good faith to be cyber bullying, even if the term wasn't in vogue as yet. This was certainly not unique to my students or my school even then. Today, the numbers of students who, on a daily basis in our classrooms across the country, are using their cell phones and other devices to post video and pictures of their peers, their teachers, and themselves doing everything from the most benign, legitimate activities to sleeping in class or, worse, highly inappropriate and even dangerous activities, would absolutely astound everyone if they actually knew the realities as they exist.

And so the reality check is that, regardless of how we *want* technology to be used in the classroom, kids are using it in ways that we cannot and, in most cases, *should* not attempt to control.

Why do I say "should not"? The problem is that schools place limits on cellphone use in school, requiring that cameras be disabled, forbidding student use of text messages or Facebook, and so on. But the flaw with this approach is that, while limiting the bad behaviors that may take place in the classroom, once the student with a cell phone walks into the hallway, the lunchroom, or anywhere else on school grounds, the students can access any site, any tool, or any resource they want.

By taking the lock-it-all-down approach, the schools are throwing the baby out with the bathwater and keeping students from exploiting the positive aspects of that same technology.

I would go a step further and say that we have a moral and ethical obligation to teach students how to navigate the internet in the same way that we have spent decades and millions of dollars teaching young children about "stranger danger" and young adults everything about the dangers associated with risky behavior.

These are difficult seas to navigate. Though cyber bullying has attracted a lot of attention, there is a lack of clarity, and very little consistency, when it comes to the laws on bullying and how they relate to the very real problem of cyber bullying. According to the Cyberbullying Research Center (cyberbullying.us), at least 44 states currently have anti-bullying laws on the books. Six of those states' laws include language that specifically mentions cyber bullying, while another 31 states have anti-bullying laws that specifically mention "electronic harassment." But how much schools can count on the law to *prevent* the bad behavior rather than punish it after the fact is truly uncertain.

Sometimes constraining behavior actually runs counter to what communities want for their children. For instance, while limiting access to the web in schools may be seen as a way to keep children from engaging in risky online behavior, the truth may well be the opposite. My experience as a virtual school administrator leads me to believe that those students who are given the opportunity to utilize digital tools such as message centers, wikis, collaboration sites or community boards, and participating in webinars are actually *less* likely to engage in poor behavior online.

One of the worst examples of technology in our schools today is probably the most common. Let's take the school that advertises a great one-to-one iPad or tablet initiative. For the most part, these schools have rendered the iPad virtually useless as a teaching tool and, in fact, the iPads (or any of the other tablets out there which have the capacity to really do good things in the classroom) are relegated to being little more than updated typewriters.

Instead of fully exploiting the devices' multimedia potentials, teachers all across the country are using the tablets to perform functions that could just as easily be performed by using e-mail; transmitting a list of work or assignments, and displaying material.

Very rarely are students permitted to use features such as the recording features to actually create work, so it's inaccurate to blame the technology for the failings of how it's been implemented. In truth, the fault lies with a system that handicaps educators with near-insurmountable fear of the ramifications of potential lawsuits for what might happen if a small minority of students were to use the technology inappropriately.

But by telling students a particular kind of activity has no legitimate use, it encourages them to think of that activity as only being something recreational and frivolous, if not outright illicit.

It's safe to say that the majority of students currently in a classroom using iPads or other tablets have no real interest in using the school-issued tablet for anything, including their work, because we have turned the use of the device into such a chore, that we have taken away the excitement or "hook" that we might actually have used to get them engaged in their own learning.

The kids I know who are using a school-issued iPad or device look on it as a burden, because they cannot use their own social media, apps, or anything that has meaning or relevance in their life on the device. In fact, many of these learners can't figure out why they are carrying the device *plus* their textbooks, when neither connects with how they

28

engage in learning, researching, gaming, or community building online.

And therein I can predict with the greatest of ease that "this too shall pass" and the tablets fad will be remembered as one of those cool things we did during this decade, but they will not in any way lead to a new way of teaching and learning, *unless* we do something immediately to ensure that the injection of devices into the classroom is accompanied by real reform.

I would go so far as to say that there will actually be schools and districts who will invest in tablets, issue them to their students, and get rid of them before they've really had time to impact learning.

The beginnings of individual institutional attempts at reform are emerging. We are seeing schools that combine "bricks" — the solid structures and communitarian virtues of a dedicated school building — with "clicks" the use of computers for research, attending virtual classes, and collaborating with fellow students on classwork. There are a number of outstanding models already popping up around the country where this blending of education delivery and learning modalities are beginning to be successful. These hybrid schools can make maximum use of student potential and encourage them to use the commonplace tools of the digital age in a positive way.

The concern is that these blended learning approaches applied to the old model make only superficial improvements while reiterating or exacerbating all the old problems.

The Christensen Institute (www.christenseninstitute.org) defines blended learning as "a formal education program in which a student learns at least in part through the online delivery of content and instruction, with some element of student control over time, place, path, and/or pace, and at least in part at a supervised brick-and-mortar location away from home." Beyond simply providing devices for students, blended learning includes a deliberate shift to online instructional delivery for a portion of the day in order to boost student, teacher, and school productivity.

6 Special Sauce

Too often, the way state and local governments prove that they are serious about education reform is by declaring that certain schools have failed. But this stigma of failure doesn't help anyone. Closing schools doesn't help communities stay stable, and declaring that teachers have failed doesn't encourage these educators — many of whose "failures" were the results of a lack of systemic support — to do their best work and find ways to innovate on behalf of their students. As a result, these "failed schools" fail even further and no one benefits.

One response to the perceived failures of public schools over the past decade has been the rapid rise of the charter school movement.

One of the primary ways charter schools differ from traditional schools is the lack of governmental oversight and other restrictive policies. That's a very simplistic differentiation, but, even so, it is enough to actually make a difference. (Often the charters use the same teachers as the public schools, educators whose training had supposedly been found insufficient to the task at hand during their tenure in the public school system, so for the most part I'm going to make a huge deduction and assume the performance of the individual educators is not really the reason for the poor public school performance.)

On the other hand, charters and private schools alike have found much success by embracing new ideas and being flexible in their approach. For instance, they have been among the first to embrace the idea of blended learning.

Where austerity-level financing and union backed tenure systems have forced public schools to lay off the last-hired teachers — typically non-veteran educators with greater affinity for the technology of the digital age — that talent base has found a home in newly launched charters and private schools, places where younger talent can be picked up because it costs less and there are no tenure concerns. The curriculum has adapted accordingly.

It is in these charter and private schools that we are seeing the most innovation, the least resistance to change, and indeed the most rapid transition to blended learning, because they can make decisions and respond to needs quickly.

It is this flexibility and adaptability that is missing from our public school system, the capacity for administrators to make decisions that are meaningful, relevant, and timely without fear and without the shackles of over-bureaucratized leadership.

Another, unsurprising, reaction to the problems in public schools has been an increase in homeschooling. The homeschool isn't new — it's really the most classic form of education, one where lesson plans and areas of study are more individualized than in any other formal structure — and of course it provides the kind of one-to-one ratio between teachers and students that no public school could ever match (imagine the taxes you'd have to pay for that) and no private school could attempt without charging tuition that only Bill Gates could afford. Parents have the most direct interest in their specific child's education, while public-school teachers are challenged to provide any child much in the way of individual attention and often have little choice but to teach to the group rather than the individual.

What is significant is what's different about the new model of homeschooling. Gone are the days of homeschools being associated only with families who want to keep their children away from the dangers of discipline problems or poor academic performance associated with public schools. Gone too is the notion that homeschool families are religious fanatics who want to control what their children are exposed to in the public-school curriculum. Gone are the days of the parent (or a cohort of parents) being the only provider of information, using a textbook which was mailed to the house.

What has transformed the homeschool education of today is ironically the same technology that has been so restricted in the public-school setting.

Because public policy in many states dictates that homeschool students have access to the same resources provided to students attending public schools, in the days of virtual education this means that the homeschool student now has the best of both worlds: access to online classes, including everything from core curriculum, electives, advanced placement or dual-enrollment college-credit classes, along with all the resources associated with that access, but the total flexibility to take the classes any time of the day or week, in the comfort and safety of their own home, while on family vacations, or in any other setting.

Other than the need for a babysitter or someone to supervise younger students, who on earth would not want the flexibility of having their children learn whenever they want to learn, whatever they want to learn, to be free from the hassles of state-mandated testing, and still have the opportunity to participate in activities, services, or other opportunities at the taxpayer expense?

Given that, why on earth do we handicap our public schools and teachers in ways that we do not begin to burden our charter our homeschool environments?

All the different approaches — charter school, private school, and homeschool — claim to have found the "special sauce" that makes their version the best at unlocking teacher capacity and student potential. But the really special thing is what they all share: the ability to function without bureaucracy and act as real, competitive educational environments.

Certainly public schools are incredibly hampered by governmental bureaucracy and, frankly, the requirement that they educate every student who comes through the door (whether those students want to be educated or not), but there's a fallacy that the "failed school" notion promulgates: the toxic notion that all public schools are terrible and all public-school teachers and administrators are terrible. This is categorically not true.

The challenge is to find ways to remove roadblocks to improving public schools.

Whether those roadblocks are, among other things, overly conservative or undereducated school boards; penny-wise, pound-foolish legislatures; or intransigent unions, reform measures are essential for future success.

One very impressive example of an effort to cut through the Gordian knot that strangles innovation can be found in Digital Learning Now!, (DLN) a bipartisan effort headed by former Florida governor Jeb Bush and former West Virginia governor Bob Wise. Their goal is to train legislators to better understand what's necessary to craft laws that can reform the educational system at every level, and provide research-backed findings that can help those legislators better make the case for reform to parents, administrators, and teachers.

DLN bases much of their blueprint for change on the inarguable truth that the results of the status quo in education have been dismal; going on to find that one of the major disconnects between academia and life outside of school is the use of the web. Teens who have grown up with e-readers and smartphones and web-enabled personal computers are rightly called "digital natives," and those natives see digital interaction and learning as a way of life everywhere they go, except the classroom, where their familiar technologies for learning and exploring are either taken away or brutally and arbitrarily constrained.

Digital Learning Now! argues strongly in favor of a cost-effective approach to blended learning, which is defined for their purposes as incorporating "an intentional shift of instruction to an online or technology-based environment. This innovation approach effectively incorporates engaging lessons, adaptive curriculum, virtual environments, and learning games on Web 2.0 platforms, which boost learning. At the same time, this model allows differentiated and distributed staffing which saves money and extends the reach of effective teachers by allowing them to teach more students in smaller, more personalized settings."

The DLN website (www.digitallearningnow.com) is a terrific resource for state rankings on digital-learning initiatives. Giving letter grades based on ten criteria — student eligibility, student access, personalized learning, advancement, quality content, quality instruction, quality choices, assessment and accountability, funding, and delivery — the site offers a clear apples-to-apples comparison of efforts across the country.

Excellent case studies of what can be done on the state and local level can be found in my home state of Florida.

Let's take a look at one of the large Florida public school districts. The statewide public virtual school, FLVS, has been an exemplary model of online education, serving students both statewide and outside of the state of Florida for almost a decade. Bruce Friend, Julie Young and the original team were, and still are, pioneers in doing fabulous things for virtual and blended learning! An example of the adaptation by a public district can be seen in Duval County Public Schools (DCPS), which opened its doors to virtual education in 2009, largely due to the Florida Legislation requiring full time Virtual Instruction Programs (VIP) in every school district to serve students in grades 9-12.

Upon finalization of legislation, DCPS immediately contracted with providers to implement full-time virtual education, serving approximately 200 students. In January of 2010, Dr. Marilyn Myers returned to her home district to serve as Principal for the Virtual Instruction Program. It was under her leadership and forward thinking that she transformed the VIP from contract providers to a district-supervised, school-based virtual model.

Developing the Duval Virtual Instruction Academy (DVIA), she completely staffed the new school model and worked to contract with providers that would allow the district to use its own teachers and align the VIP requirements with the district model of excellent education for all.

Since 2010, Duval Virtual Instruction Academy has not only developed a solid foundation of serving 300-500 full time students on an annual basis, but is also supporting the district in meeting the new legislative requirements regarding class size, blended learning, and high-school graduation.

Since August of 2013, there has been a significant change in the model being offered, including a full implementation process to meet the graduation requirement of one virtual credit by introducing blended learning in every high school within the district. Using specific courses when possible, and adapting to school needs, DVIA could serve over 7,000 students by the end of the 2013-2014 school year.

Duval County is not alone in implementing the "do-it-yourself" model of delivering blended and virtual learning.

Many of the other districts are following suit, and are building models for instruction and funding that can be used as a template for public education across the country.

Obviously, the long-term impact of the Florida legislation is yet to be seen, but it is certainly a courageous and bold step toward supporting public education by providing legislative and innovative funding channels that create opportunities for districts to run their own digital environments. I predict that Florida will see a reduction in the number of virtual students taking classes in schools operated by private corporations or the state virtual school, but will see a significant increase, and even exponential growth, in the numbers of students taking advantage of the educational choices being offered through blended learning innovations.

But as much as attempts have been made to achieve reform goals within the current framework, and indeed, the Florida legislation is well ahead of the curve, there is still much work to be done.

As we consider how to change the laws that shape our classroom environments and try to tailor curricula to reflect the realities of student life and how these students navigate the increasingly digital world, we quickly come to another fundamental understanding that must be reevaluated if we have any hope of reforming and rebuilding education: how do we define "school"?

7 What does "school" mean?

I've spent some time here discussing the idea of the failing school, and how the paradigm of labeling or closing those schools doesn't work. The last thing *any* community needs, at any income level, is closing schools. What may be closer to reality — and may offer a prescription for treating some of our systemic problems — is that the criteria used to evaluate schools may not be relevant to today's educational needs and ought to be revised accordingly.

No matter how many advantages are offered by virtual classrooms — and I'm a big believer in virtual schooling — students derive real value from physical, in-person school experiences in their home communities.

While the need for traditional, sprawling brick-and-mortar school campuses may not be what it once was, that doesn't mean we discard the idea of a school as a real-world location to which students travel on any given day. What may change, however, is how often the students go to the building, what kinds of activities they engage in when they get there, and yes, even what the building itself looks like in the years to come.

As I've already discussed, schools have connoted different structures over time. The one-room brick schoolhouse that educated the children of farmers from all over a given county, but only for a few days a week — and even then only during seasons when the child labor could be spared from bringing in crops — was supplanted by the five-days-a-week schools whose calendar had little to do with the needs of a farming cycle.

But as with so many other aspects of the educational system, we've by and large allowed the idea of what a school is to freeze in place for the better part of a century. Certainly a school can be a brick-and-mortar structure, with classes running all day long, and that probably makes a good deal of sense in densely populated urban areas.

On the other hand, one-to-one devices can be useful to students even as early as the kindergarten level, and virtual classes can take place inside the school to link students to specialized classes with instructors based hundreds or even *thousands* of miles away.

In communities that are geographically spread out and have low populations, Advanced Placement or AP-level students who might not have had access to high-quality AP classes in their own community can now have access to AP classes that can be offered anywhere, any time. A district might only have one AP-level student in a certain discipline, but today's technology can provide that student access to the best teacher in the subject *anywhere*.

But it goes even further than that.

In the same way that the web has enabled young people to form virtual communities of friends with similar interests in distant cities, states, and even countries, this technology can create specialized schools to meet the needs of students who might be isolated by physical or ideological circumstances.

In Pueblo, Colorado, a community that had not been able to support a Catholic high school based on its geographical area in more than fifty years, a web-enabled effort has created a virtual high-school experience for students from around the state. Superintendent John Brainard began the process four years ago by keeping his graduating eighth grade students from the Catholic K-8 program on the church grounds in a portable building. This small group of students formed the first cohort and actually graduated the first high school student in June 2013 through a partnership with a virtual school program. This process has been repeated in multiple states with multiple schools in recent years.

The infusion of virtual education into brick-and-mortar schools and programs has allowed small schools and districts to offer courses for different ages as well as enrichment, supplemental education, credit recovery, and advanced courses, and has provided many other unforeseen opportunities as well.

In Jemez Mountain School District, New Mexico, Dr. Manuel Medrano and his team have launched a digital initiative using laptops and online curriculum to provide high quality innovative educational experiences to children and families whom the American public at large would never believe were engaged in one-to-one blended learning for the past few years. Despite infrastructure concerns of the region, their three schools are hot beds of active students learning using a wide variety of resources, tools and all supported by dedicated and motivated educators.

In the case of the small school, whether private, public, or charter, it is not cost effective to try to operate a homegrown model of virtual education as an independent venture. This is where we will see an

41

increased number of consortia or public-private partnerships expanding. The new model must allow additional buying power, staffing, and all the necessary supports to be shared across schools and organizations. With this conglomerate, or educational support services network development, it will be necessary to rethink both the traditional budgets and services in order to provide for economies of scale, and the delegation of control or authority to utilize such budgets in a new way.

It's not just religious education or small schools that stand to benefit from this approach. In an era of austerity-driven cuts to anything that seems frivolous, programs such as the arts in public schools often seem like they're on an endangered-species list, especially in communities where the tax base might not be able to provide the resources for all the programs a parent might want for his or her child, virtual communities can provide supplemental arts education across a wider area than any local school could offer, for a fraction of the cost.

STEAM programs — the name comes from the idea of adding the Arts to the Science-Technology-Engineering - Math curriculum — make the case for finding room for the arts in students' lives. Given what I've already argued in terms of refocusing the school experience on training students towards jobs in the modern economy, you might expect me to argue that arts education is an indulgence we can't afford, but that's not the case at all.

Arts education is invaluable because we want to build all sides of the student's brain, to help them become adults who can carry on a conversation, communicate effectively, understand cultural needs and nuances, speak different languages, and who can appreciate music, theatre, etc.

The arts are a way to understand other people's interests and viewpoints, which is key to building consensus and working in teams. Arts education helps students learn how to develop relationships in all sorts of interpersonal areas, which can translate into every level of the workplace from customer service to design teams, and will stimulate creativity and innovation. And while the local brick-and-mortar school might not have room for the arts, the virtual classroom can bring the arts into education in a meaningful, relevant, and modern way.

We cannot take every child in the country to the Smithsonian, but we certainly can bring the Smithsonian to every child in the country using an online experience. The same goes for the opera, the ballet, and all of those cultural opportunities formerly reserved for the affluent and those in more metropolitan areas to experience.

8 Parents just don't understand?

Any effort to reform education will be made immeasurably more difficult if parents (whose votes in state and local government elections have a big impact on schools) aren't on board. It's also worth mentioning that the ever-growing charter, private and homeschooling population who have all chosen to remove their children from public schools means there is an ever-growing population that does not have American public schools on the top of its priority list for funding or anything else. And enlisting their aid can be a real challenge, especially as the kind of radical change we're talking about here will probably have little impact on students who are already pretty far along in their educational life-cycle. Imagine telling the parent of a high-school freshman "sorry, it's too late for Tommy, but if you have a newborn, she's got a real shot if we pass this legislation... be sure to vote, okay?"

Let's try to think past the resistance parents often offer to schools that don't resemble what they encountered in their day.

When schools were turning out graduates to populate a working- and middle-class workforce whose jobs were in sprawling factories or giant, *Mad Men*-era offices, it made sense to educate children in orderly, uniform rows of desks. But today's open-space, collaborative workplace

44

doesn't reflect the straight lines, desks-all-in-a-row format we grew up with in our education.

Additionally, parents' perception of what schools are supposed to be doesn't line up with the challenge of engaging today's youth, who spend 70-80 percent of their time online, using their thumbs to navigate the web on their phones or tablets.

This year's class of kindergarteners will likely be the first generation of students who will never use a keyboard in their lives due to touch screens and high-tech eyewear or even (I kid you not) brain implants, so we have to make sure that they don't see the classroom as a step backwards from the high-tech environments where they spend their non-school time. And we're already falling behind on that score. According to one study, while 94% of students use technology at home, only 46% of teachers give assignments that require it.

Where a student in the 1970s might have pecked out a term paper on a manual typewriter and one in the 1980s used an electric, we're now seeing the transition between reports being printed out from home computers to a time when students now skip the printout stage entirely. Even if the students are submitting their homework in more advanced ways than was the norm even a few years ago, taking blue-book essay exams or multiple-choice tests once they are in the classroom just reinforces a sense that school is an outmoded anachronism with little relevance to the students' lives.

While the paperless office has remained an unfulfilled promise, the paperless classroom might actually become a reality in the coming years, but only if we have the courage of our convictions and make the sweeping changes needed to reinvent our children's schools, even if the result is an environment wildly different from what we experienced in our own youth. Changes in schools over the years have been subtle, but dramatic change is not merely crucial, I'd say it's mission-critical to any reform of the educational system.

9   The teacher in the palm of your hand

Traditionally, the teacher has been the students' main purveyor of knowledge, but, as we've already discussed, the Internet contains more "knowledge" than any teacher, and is accessible to students anytime, anywhere.

Everything we know in our understanding of the teacher at a lectern at the front of the room has been knocked off its axis by students' access to technology that is getting smaller, faster, smarter, and less expensive by the day. And as it becomes more ubiquitous, there really is no turning back.

Today, the common person — regardless of age or formal-education level — has access to more information (quality not under discussion at this time) about everything than any expert could provide. Doctors, lawyers, real-estate agents, and professionals at almost every level have seen their businesses radically impacted by this truism, and educators are no exception.

So what is the new role of the teacher?

As we consider the new teacher-to-student equation, we should pay attention to the positives. On the plus side, students now have their curiosity rewarded (and encouraged) about everything; from apps that tell them the name of a song they hear on an elevator or in a store, to Google or Wikipedia answering any question they have about, well, almost anything.

47

On the other hand, these shortcuts to knowledge teach nothing about patience or about conducting truly rigorous, primary-source research, and fail to help students identify and properly weigh the dubious information and digital chaff that dominate the web.

Teachers need to help curate the students' travels through the web, helping them avoid searches that lead them down the proverbial rabbit hole, educating them on things that are, at best, off-topic and, at worst, wildly inaccurate. But that role isn't enough for our students, and would be a waste of the personal capital and talent offered by our best educators.

As the classroom experience is infused with new technology, instructing teachers on best practices to utilize that technology effectively is an often-neglected step in modernizing the classroom. It is time to rethink and revitalize teaching as a profession to properly reflect its role in a complex, 21st century world.

While trying to figure out new ways to empower students to use different kinds of tools, teachers have been left out in the cold completely or left to play catch-up without much in the way of new support. We need to ask ourselves what being an effective educator means in a modern context and we need to ensure our teachers are appropriately prepared for their new role. I recently spoke with a number of colleagues at iNACOL's annual conference, the Virtual and Blended Learning Symposium, and one of those experts shared a provocative thought:

"With the shift towards greater utilization of digital content and online/blended instruction, one important part of the learning equation however remains the same - the need for highly skilled teachers who excel in the ability to support, mentor, and build positive working relationships with students. Just as technology is a catalyst for accomplishing tasks more efficiently and effectively in so many phases of our everyday life, so too does technology have the power to increase student interest and achievement in school. Technology will not replace teachers in schools, be they online, blended, or traditional schools; however, teachers who use technology will replace those who do not. In many ways this is inevitable; in terms of making learning more relevant, fun, and engaging for students, the time for this to occur is now." (Bruce Friend – former C.O.O. for FLVS, Vice-president iNACOL, and currently President, Friend Consulting.)

Firstly, we need to better and more clearly define expectations for teachers and leaders. Let me clearly state that we are not talking about training teachers or leaders how to use devices or software. That is a given, knowing that schools everywhere have already, and will continuously repeat that type of training every time we change the gadgets and gizmos that are identified as the new technologies of the day. Statewide communication systems need to be improved, as do better articulated and executed standards for training. While training for leadership needs to be rethought, the unfortunate reality is that very few "experts" who would lead these trainings are actually practitioners or experienced in the large-scale implementation of reform on a systemic scale. In simple terms this means that while there are a growing number of theorists, there are very few people who will be able to share replicable strategies in the near future.

We need thousands of well-prepared, highly savvy teachers and support staff who teach in school organizations designed to facilitate sharing their expertise with colleagues down the hall as well as in virtual communities.

These teachers, either alone or in small groups, have to be encouraged to find and engage with the professional learning that is relevant for their practice. In the same way teachers must be able to use devices for assessing ongoing student performance, the administrators should be able to use apps for smartphones and tablets or handheld devices for classroom walk-throughs, which allow users to collect data on classes and upload it for later analysis. This capacity to analyze teacher performance and student performance is already in operation in the virtual-school environment. Capturing this capacity to make teacher evaluations, and subsequent teacher support, relevant is a critical step. And it's not just the teacher evaluation process that needs updated.

The reform of processes through technology needs to infiltrate every aspect of our services to staff and to students.

Other ways school services can evolve and improve in the digital age include simple but effective offerings for students in the K-12 environment. Easy to implement strategies like offering online counseling sessions for students, which can utilize real-time status updates of performance and effort and offer guidance when it's needed, rather than waiting for the results of tests and other reports to be reviewed at scheduled intervals. Over a decade ago, I worked with a really great Director of Guidance in a public school. Ken Orban and his team of counselors began offering what was then described as "a smorgasbord of guidance services" during lunchtime periods. Complete with twenty-foot tall menu boards showing a la carte lunchtime counseling services, they put standup kiosks with computers into the cafeteria so that thousands of students had access to their counselor "on lunch duty" to be able to take care of all of those things that can be resolved with a simple, five-minute conversation and access to a computer, small things that would otherwise mean students missing an hour of class or waiting a week for an appointment.

While certainly ahead of its time, this "counselor on demand" service-oriented, technology infused high school counseling model is still a great concept today.

But more importantly, it is an example of what can happen in our public schools when we empower people who know the needs and requirements of their jobs to actually do their jobs in ways that they know can best meet the needs of their individual "student clients" rather than forcing old models on staff because "that's how we've always done it."

Again, most of today's staff evaluation rubrics do not take into account enough of the spirit of innovation and the implementation of these great child-centric models implemented by caring professionals empowered to do their jobs. I applaud the work of those pioneers who are trying to create much needed new models for systemic teacher evaluation.

Using technology today, faculty members can send personalized communications that offer detailed guidance around major areas for improvement. Students can then choose to contact the instructor directly and/or access suggested resources, and there are many great products on the market today for engaging students in career or college goal-setting, traits analysis, and other career-oriented activities. Having more options for how to proceed makes the student more of an active participant in improving their performance, taking ownership for their learning.

Digital curriculum guides are an obvious part of modernizing the teaching experience, but virtual technology can go beyond that. Areas of the traditional school such as the library have long been described as the "hub" of the school. The librarian has been in the precarious, ever-changing role of being not only the one to manage and control the distribution of reading materials and teacher resources, but also being a full-time teacher of media studies in the days when budgets did not allow for a full-time, dedicated librarian position.

With today's technologies, the role of the librarian or media specialist is changing once again. The media specialist of today truly provides an opportunity for a dynamic school digital environment to exist. The skill set of the media specialist requires someone who can teach children not only how to use technologies, but also who can teach and support teachers in their mission to provide a high-tech, high-quality digital environment for the students. It is very often the media specialist, particularly in the elementary schools, who works with every adult and every child on the campus. What an incredible opportunity this person has to make a difference and to impact the future of learning.

I hear immediately the groaning of some of you who don't believe that the old-fashioned "Madame Librarian" is capable of change. I've got to share an experience, one where such a librarian worked for me at a time when we were building a high-tech professional learning community in a large public high school for teachers, while trying to implement smaller learning communities for the students.

Through a great relationship with Troy Williams, then CEO and President of Questia, our school team worked with Questia Online Library and Questia Classroom, the first course management system (CMS) to be attached to a vast scholarly collection of full-text copyrighted and public-domain material. Again, ahead of her time, this school librarian, Diane Zukowski, was definitely a pioneer in being able to not only embrace the implementation of a model of what Williams described as "the modern classroom thriving on interaction and collaboration among students, teachers, and technology," but was able to lead discussions with her peers who were not so sure that a new way of doing business was coming.

There is much to be done in defining the new role of the media specialist or school librarian for digital age schools. This will range from identifying whether or not the role demands a technology guru, a literacy specialist, a curriculum leader, or indeed a combination of all of the above.

There is no doubt that teacher quality can be improved by online professional development and a teacher commons, sort of like a teachers' lounge crossed with a password-protected chat room and a shared repository of assets and learning objects.

Much as students can benefit from interacting with like-minded kids from a wider geographical area, so too can teachers benefit from professional collaboration with other educators beyond their physical school.

Using online tools, teachers can more easily collaborate with students to develop lesson plans that serve the students' educational needs while simultaneously engaging them in a way that is relevant to their modern lives.

As schools consider what students need to learn, how students learn and what we expect them to do with the knowledge gained is a salient question.

Without getting into an entire discussion on ways to teach reading across the curriculum, infusing technology into the process is imperative.

As e-readers become more commonplace, texts that have embedded hyperlinks to related areas of study and interest have also become more common, paving the way for the use of digital textbooks. But even then, teachers are needed to steer any given student's journey around the aforementioned rabbit holes.

Another key area where the infusion of virtual education into the traditional schedule can transform the school experience for students and teachers alike is in offering more flexible office hours, classroom hours, and even online-only summer school, either as a catch-up for students that have fallen behind, or as an option for advanced students who hope to matriculate more quickly.

But finding a way for overstressed school budgets to pay for teachers and other staff to work longer hours and more days is going to increasingly become more of a major challenge.

10 Where are these new-model teachers?

As briefly discussed, the truly effective modern teacher is unlikely to rate well on the majority of evaluation scales used in the United States today because those scales don't recognize the newer skills as something to evaluate.

The traditional teacher-evaluation rubric in most cases is one which captures the essence of the teacher's performing as "sage on the stage," and so provides appropriate check-offs when the teacher delivers content, asks appropriate questions, asks questions in the "correct" format, walks around the room monitoring the students and preventing negative behaviors, and praises children for giving appropriate responses at the appropriate time.

In effect, the majority of teacher-evaluation tools being used by today's schools and districts have no way to capture, and may even find tremendous fault with, the teacher who is truly dynamic in the blended learning classroom of today.

There is no place "on the form" being used by the administrators while walking around a classroom to identify the teacher who can multitask, engage students in digital differentiated instruction, and make use of a wide variety of digital assets to supplement and enhance classroom learning. In fact, today's highly successful classrooms might well look chaotic and noisy, as they will include students using their headsets and cellphones (and other devices) along with nonconventional seating arrangements; and will incorporate virtual interactions with students outside the physical space. And the teacher certainly is not at her desk, as she is much too busy being the conductor of the orchestra that is today's innovative classroom.

The teacher I'm talking about must be someone who *facilitates learning*. And while that phrase has the ring of a sort of New Age-y sounding buzzword that connotes laziness at worst and something impossible to quantify at best, it shouldn't. It's a concrete concept that includes the skill set the teacher needs as well as the time on task the teacher needs to provide.

For years we've talked about education going from a teacher-centric model to a student-centric one, but in actuality it has to drill down further than that, to become a focus on the *learning process* for *each individual*.

However, this should not be confused with a move towards kids driving the learning process, directing classroom activities themselves while teachers move away from lectures to some sort of supervisory role.

Today's teacher has to understand how everything in the process impacts learning and how each individual child learns. This shift to personalized learning ends the era where a teacher could tell students to read things off a board, turn to a given page in their textbooks, and then just hope that the knowledge replicates in the students' brains.

Over the next five to ten years, either teachers are going to become innovative, embracing their role as instruments of change and the driving force of their own

educational revolution, or their existing model will become obsolete as a profession, replaced by "super/master teachers" with subject-area specialists and supports.

The goal here isn't some sort of "computer-based instruction" with teachers serving as tech support; rather, we're talking about managing how students move through a personalized curriculum. A skilled educator can monitor not only what the kids are learning, but also what path they're taking to get to the information, steering them away from distractions so they can master concrete, valuable skills.

There are indeed pockets of innovation around the United States, and the numbers of schools and innovative educational leaders who are willing to try new things during this era of blended learning is on the rise. There are school networks that pride themselves on innovation, blended-learning efforts, public/private partnerships and much more, all in an effort to get better results for student performance. In each of these cases, steps have been made to blend the use of technology into the curriculum, and to use the data captured to provide individualized learning plans for each student.

The use of the "flipped classroom" is already seeing significant growth across the country. It's a concept that encourages students to read the text, watch video tutorials, and pursue a multitude of other independent study activities at home or outside the classroom experience while leaving classroom time for engaging with the teacher and with peers in higher-order critical-thinking types of activities.

The flexibility that comes with blended learning and flipping our classrooms means that students and

teachers get to extend the teachable hours while increasing the quality of classroom face-to-face time, since it can now be presumed the students already have a knowledge of the content, and can focus on the key area of "what we want the learner to do with that content" instead.

A greater need for collaboration between teachers and students requires a greater role for the teacher in students' lives. It also emphasizes the significance of the gaps which will rapidly occur between the students who have access 24-7 and those who go home to environments which are tech-poor, but that's another discussion. In a world where students can learn and explore 24-7, teachers have to be more available, with online weekend and nighttime office hours a likely development unless we get to the point of 24 hour staffing in shifts.

And herein lies another new role for teacher unions and other support organizations. Instead of fighting over the things that they have traditionally argued for, educational organizations should be working directly at the federal and state level to begin to craft what the new working conditions and expectations are for a modern teacher.

This is much too important a discussion to be left to chance, and therefore should not be left up to individual local school districts or private schools to define. I know there are those who will immediately scream that education is not the federal government's job, and I agree completely, but the support for local education authorities to implement change must be on

such a scale that it will take funding and legislation at the national level if it is to be successful system wide.

We are talking about the most significant and major overhaul of the industry of teaching. It cannot be simply about paychecks and time off, it must be an all-inclusive and systemic reform of the industry, and must include input from all stakeholders.

If today's teachers are to begin to change how they do their core business, they must receive all the tools of the trade, which means complete retraining on using the tools of today. It includes being given personal access to those technologies for 24-7 use, and may include things that we've never considered for teachers before, such as providing home-based Internet stipends, personal laptops, tablets, and stipends for resources to use within our classrooms. It must include a complete revamp of teacher compensation, as well.

Reform must allow for massive numbers of teachers to be shared across buildings and disciplines, and the breaking down of many jurisdictional boundaries.

Consideration for models such as those allowing the Higher-Ed model of adjunct faculty to expand as a way of doing business in the K-12 space should be discussed. It will also involve massive retraining of education professionals. All too often, teachers receive 10 to 20 hours of training at the beginning of the school year, a couple of hours each month dedicated to in-service, and, for those who are committed to their own professional growth, they pay for advanced degrees or other college-level courses themselves.

One of the key factors that need to be taken into consideration is that when we move into a model of blended learning, it allows us to begin to use the technologies available to gather data on student and teacher performance alike. There are many great platforms in the industry today, ranging from a variety of first-generation or simple learning-management systems to those that aggregate rich content and gather data on student engagement with media. Regardless of the brand, the tools are becoming increasingly more affordable, and are capable of complex data analysis.

The data gathered in our classrooms today can include information about the content, about the teacher, and about how the student measures up on a number of metrics, including time on task, educational standard, grade-level standards, content type, media type, level of rigor, and much more. With this in mind, today's educator will need extensive training on how best to utilize this data, to analyze the information generated from these complex learning systems, and all the implications of how massive amounts of data can inform us about how our students are actually learning.

Modern technology can also be used to enhance parental involvement in their children's education in a way far more meaningful than just using email to send home report cards or using Google calendar to schedule a parent-teacher conference. Even brick-and-mortar schools can create a parent portal that enables parents, no matter how busy, to be an active participant in the student-teacher relationship.

Many of us are fortunate to at least have access to our children's grades and attendance information online. Gone are the days of the student trying to beat the parent home to erase the phone message from the school that was left on the answering machine. Today's parents can login any time or place, during the lunch hour, from the office, from the public library, or from their cellphone, and in most cases access student grades real-time, and usually see attendance and discipline information as recorded by the school.

In schools that have started using blended learning initiatives and modern student-information systems which have been designed specifically for the K-12 environment, parents today have access to lessons and curricula, video tutorials, or other web-based resources in use by the teacher, as well as interactive whiteboards, communication logs, message centers, and the ability to have e-mail communications with all members of their children's educational team. While this means parents can and should become increasingly involved in their children's education, it also places a tremendous burden on the school system to ensure that all parents have equity of access to the information that can create a vital difference in how their child is educated, and in how they respond to meeting the needs of the school. Meeting this obligation will require a tremendous change in the average hours worked by every professional involved in the education of the learner, as well as when those hours take place in the day.

Clearly, if we want teachers to be on-call all the time, training, pay scales, structures, and evaluations will all need to be redefined accordingly.

How seniority and tenure work will also need to be re-examined in light of the changing skills teachers will be required to learn and master. This will require efforts on the local, state, and federal level.

Just as our K-12 schools' curricula are being wildly outpaced by developments in technology, so too the vast majority of teacher-education programs aren't able to keep up with advances in technology available to those students striving to become teachers. Unfortunately or fortunately, depending upon who you speak with, there are changes taking place within Higher Ed simultaneously with the changes in K-12 education that are frightening and exciting at the same time for the college and university stakeholders. These same advances in blended learning are beginning to sweep across the University system, and while some would argue that technology and distance education are no stranger to Higher Ed, where some institutions have been delivering virtual education, using a variety of modalities, for 50 years, this is probably the first time that the framework of higher education is being shaken up.

There are the naysayers out there who will undoubtedly believe that the use of MOOCs will never replace the lecturer, but the reality is that even our most prestigious universities will have to face the fact that innovation in education will significantly transform the best of practices at all levels of teaching and learning. The data is already in, and we know that online education coupled with some face-to-face contact can actually help students to master content better than if they had gone to a classroom only.

A big question is how fast teacher education schools can adapt to prepare the next generation of teachers, and support the transformation necessary for existing teachers to be able to work in this new environment.

Those colleges of education which are not offering educators and potential educators exciting hubs of research, labs, and places where they can learn and practice their new role with colleagues in a collaborative environment will find themselves obsolete, in an era where the best content, research, teachers, and support can be found from the top colleges on the planet at the click of a button or the swipe of a touchscreen.

11 ...and how do we pay for them?

I'll be talking about the other areas of education that need to be overhauled, and how, a bit later, but the elephant in the room is how do we pay for any of this, so let's start getting into it here.

The traditional school-budgeting process is, for want of a better word, ridiculous. It would never be considered for any other business. There is currently no budget process that allows for innovation and creativity, unless there is a budget surplus, and the system is designed to basically penalize schools for having a surplus, so surpluses are, to put it mildly, rare.

The need to reform this so-called budgeting process is profound. The starting point for the process cannot be (and yes, I'm oversimplifying for effect) the CFO or assistant superintendent for finance beginning budget meetings with "what's the state allocating us? Are there reductions and if so you all have to cut your areas by X%, and if not, let's fund last year's programs again, and is there anything anyone needs to add if we have the budget?" Rather, the starting point should be "everything and everyone is at zero, how can we help students learn better, what are the non-negotiables that we must fund, what can help us do these things better?" and so on. Again, I know this sounds too simplistic, but most of us don't operate our home budgets in a given month based on what we did this time last year, and most companies don't set this year's budget based on what they did last year, but rather they set goals, targets and deliverables which they fund. There are just too many unfunded mandates that constrict the public school CFO and leadership team from really doing their jobs effectively as they cannot do things they'd like to be able to do.

I know that the pain points are quite simply that to do this effectively, we will have to let go of not only programs, but also people who have worked the system for years, people who have done a great job when their specific job was relevant to the old system. The problem we've already seen is that many of the jobs, titles, positions, etc., are no longer necessary functions in a blended learning environment. To perpetuate these roles, or to make minor tweaks at the system whereby we only change or modify roles-based functions when someone retires or we open a new building, results in people feeling like they are taking on all the new responsibilities and never actually losing any of the old ones. This will happen at an exponential rate, as new tasks and opportunities will require new skill sets and a complete revamping of the job descriptions we attach to educational positions today. If we choose to continue to run school finance and our human-capital management the current way, there will never be significant improvement at the local, state, or federal levels.

None of this is to say the school-based staff can't do the job under the current system, but like every other part of the educational system, the budget process just isn't set up to allow for creativity or innovation, so it makes everyone jump through arcane hoops before they can even get to finding a way to fund programs that might break the stagnant cycle we've been trapped in for generations.

A truly modern budget process would make the schools more competitive with each other in ways that represent the best of free enterprise, and allow for money-making opportunities (and no, I'm not talking about bake sales) that can be funneled back in to the school organizations to add to the resources for students.

Let's look at the dirty little word in education circles: *marketing*.

It's generally seen as unacceptable for a school district to allocate any kind of major resource for marketing dollars, the implication being that wasting money on marketing is taking dollars that could otherwise have gone to help students directly in the classroom. It's equally frowned upon when private enterprise, for-profit schools can access public dollars to provide educational services.

Let's discuss this issue. If a for-profit educational company can actually do just that, make a profit while educating students at or above the same level using the same amount of public dollars, then there's a real lesson to be learned for the public school that relates directly to the discussion of how we redesign and reprioritize funding, and the policies and practices associated with funding for public education.

I have no doubt that online education, and the implications for blended learning, will lead us to much more efficient and cost-effective ways of educating all students. It will also lead us to competition in the K-12 education space.

This is not a new concept, and certainly is not news if you consider that charter schools compete directly with the local public school and draw their FTE (full-time equivalency funding) away from that public school. Charter schools have the advantage in that they are owned and operated by private corporations or management groups which can spend dollars on creating glossy flyers, e-mail campaigns, newspaper advertising, and lots of social media to highlight the positive things going on in their schools. They can, in effect, create a buzz around their message, specifically emphasizing that children are lucky to have won the lottery draw that got them there in the first place because they are doing good things.

Virtual schools owned and operated by both public and private corporations, as well as private schools, can do the same — and often more — with regards to marketing for students than their charter-school counterparts. Some of the large companies we all know about have millions of dollars to spend each year on marketing to persuade students to take their online classes. Even the large public virtual schools have foundations or private enterprise opportunities which allow them the resources necessary to "sell their brand".

By comparison, district-run brick and mortar or virtual-school programs rely heavily on donations or other relationships with the vendors supplying them with technology, tools, textbooks, curriculum, and other resources to be able to provide even minimal collateral materials to share with their students and teachers. In some cases, the bid processes are so restricted that vendors who would normally make donations can't even give things away for free that would actually benefit the students in school programs.

It is only in our public school systems that we have removed the opportunity for a fair, competitive

process, and I don't mean a fair process for vendors, but rather we have removed the opportunity for our public schools to compete directly with the private schools, charter schools, virtual schools, and all other programs that have the capacity to market directly to the consumer who, in this case, is the student and the student's family. In some cases, the local public-school district is also competing with the local community college for the same students via dual enrollment or other adult-education programs. Bottom line is students today have options, and everyone except the local public-school system can market directly to "earn the business" of educating a student. And so the public school is reliant upon the media to tell its story.

Have you ever tried to get the press to share a good story on a busy news day? I'm not blaming the media, it's just the way it is, you all know the old saying "bad news sells" and so it's only natural that the media cannot afford to be the free public relations office for the local public school system. Besides, who wants to hear that the local public-school system is actually doing a great job?

This next piece is going to sting, but I can talk about it because I am what I am about to discuss... the lifelong educator and the story of the teacher unions. I'm a 30-year educator. I've worked in public and private schools at all levels. For my 20-plus-year tenure in the public-school system, one of the most stressful decisions I had to make as a young professional trying to move up the career ladder involved losing tenure if I took an administrative position... as a strong believer in the value of the unions to support employees in time of need and in providing a unified voice, I found myself in that strange world of being "on the outs" because administrators were not permitted as members of the teachers' union.

I later came face-to-face with the absurdity of the annual negotiating process that took place while observing the admin team sitting across from the teacher union reps and the classified workers reps. In many of the school system negotiations with the unions, everyone got the same percentage pay raises when they were negotiated, union and non-union, administrators included, so, of course, while all the usual posturing took place, the admin rep sitting across from the union rep wanted the raise just as much as the teacher (because the better-salaried admin is actually going to make more based on percentage raises), so the money for raises was never really an issue, but something had to be, right? Instead, the annual discussions often take place over planning time and training and other such items that have nothing to do with fair pay or conditions for the educators and administrators and even less to do with how to educate the students.

It seems to me that teachers picketing or striking is what contributes to the public perception that teaching is somehow less of a "real" profession than medicine or law in the eyes of the public. No matter how much empathy Joe Q. Public has with the plight of educators, that concern runs out the moment it has any negative impact on his children. Lawyers and doctors raise their rates and change other rules with impunity, but they're private businesspeople, so it's seen as a "what the market will bear" situation as opposed to people with allegedly cushy jobs — paid for by our taxes —

angling for even better treatment while the children graduate without being able to even get a job.

In the modern context of schools trying to adapt to changes that have already taken place, teacher unions will increasingly come under fire as they try to maintain the status quo in a new age and things like tenure become obsolete. In a time of rapid industry transformation, tenure becomes perceived as an attempt to keep senior employees around by giving them new tasks, regardless of whether or not their skill sets and knowledge base make them qualified to do the job.

This is in no way an attempt to suggest that the vast majority of teachers and administrators should not be retained.

In fact, some of the most dynamic educators embracing today's technologies are actually those senior and veteran teachers. And why not? They realistically see real value in, and are exploring the options of, virtual education as a way to continue in their profession while earning money in retirement from the traditional school, options which will offer many of the same things that virtual education offers to students: flexibility and the chance to work anywhere at any given time, and the opportunity to continue to grow while simultaneously meeting personal and family needs.

As already discussed, we need to look at what's needed to improve student learning, revising every job description in every school in the country, and then hire for those positions as though they've never been occupied by anyone before. In a very real way, they haven't.

70

In my humble opinion, the new role of the educational union is to take an active and aggressive stand in laying the framework for a new era, to become involved in the design and research efforts that will lead to the rebirth of the American Education System as a system that meets the needs of both the 21st century learner and the 21st century teacher.

12 People, places, spaces, and resources...

And it's not just teachers' unions that will find their status quo impacted by the new reality. Reform will have far-reaching implications, and many people whose livelihoods will be affected will be understandably defensive.

I was doing a Chamber of Commerce presentation a few months ago on my take on the failings of the current educational system and the needs for systemic reform, to an audience of non-educators. Afterwards, the President of a local construction company indicated he thought that I was "grossly underestimating" the complexity of the situation.

What he really meant was that what I was outlining the day that would threaten his business, as the need for giant high schools of the type that have been built for the last thirty-plus years would largely come to an end, and he would be forced to reduce his construction work in this area.

It makes no rational sense for our schools to be forbidding, gigantic concrete institutions that take up a city block and look like prisons or palaces; rather, we need learning centers with flexible space that offer more opportunities for community use than our current schools. Similarly, the sprawling, college-style campuses built for high schools during the 1990s are never going to be built again.

So, in addition to changing what being a teacher or an administrator means, we also have to rethink what

the physical plants for schools and colleges will look like in this new dynamic. This will breed a whole new architectural set of specs for school design, the concept of creating workspaces conducive to a new type of work environment that takes technology into consideration, as well as how students physically and mentally interact with that technology and other people in the course of learning.

In addition to providing in-classroom access to students attending remotely or online, let's consider the very-real physical changes required by a school filled with modern, digitally proficient kids utilizing technology to its utmost capacity. First of all, each and every student will have a personal device, whether rented, personal, or owned and supported by the school, causing a need for charging stations available all day, furniture appropriate to hold these devices so students can work (so no more chairs with the attached mini-tabletop), potential need for a school-based "technology support center," proper lighting to avoid impacting screens, etc.

This touches on another area where the budgeting process we discussed last chapter has to be completely reconceived. Basic assumptions, like how much electricity a school will use, and the attendant size of the budget for it, all need to be rethought. The amount of energy it took to accommodate the use of the paper and pencil for the student population 6 to 8 hours a day is radically different to the drain by those same children using technology, even *multiple* devices all day long. Please don't scream about the need for "green" buildings at me, I'm simply asking questions to make sure that the process of teaching and learning is not stopped because someone forgot to plan to pay an enormous energy bill. All joking aside, this will produce a significant difference in how we allocate for funding, and, as important, will require new skill sets of the people analyzing the school site data.

Additionally, we know our lessons will use media-rich content from multiple sources, so we need to examine the issue of adequate bandwidth for streaming media files, multiple access points, heavy internet traffic times, etc.

We've just identified *another* concern with regards to physical plant; the school's technology expert (and each school is obviously going to need more than just one) needs to operate a support center, be knowledgeable in balancing internet loads across multiple rooms and buildings, and using a wide variety of devices, browsers, and so on. This means that each school site, in addition to the district, will need access to cloud-based technologies and physical site-based hardware-maintenance spaces, plus a great relationship or set of relationships with private partners. Things just got complicated in a hurry!

And those students attending class remotely (let's say five out of every class of twenty-five) are going to need some type of audio- and video-conferencing tools incorporated into the mix, and we'll need to be able to differentiate digitally who is doing what in the classroom to be able to organize and manage the individualized pace of the students working. In a physical plant, that means creating groups, necessitating a need for a very flexible space within the room, most likely not a lab setting, as while it worked for computer-based instruction, it isn't really conducive to the new scope of digital work.

The classroom of today should reflect every administrator's nightmare with regards to supervision and liability issues. A space with nooks and crannies for students to relax with devices, lots of headsets, video cameras, open internet, pod-style conference tables, project bars full of materials for hands-on activities and labs, tiered seating to allow for presentations and demonstrations, casual areas for independent reading and discussions, and much more... it's clearly no longer enough to talk merely about bringing in new seating that's good for the back, or changing the level of the windows for optimum light.

While there may be pockets of change in facilities in individual programs, I'm looking forward to seeing the first of these learning centers appear in public education on any scale. Other than the obvious need to prepare students for the kinds of work environments they will likely be entering, there are other "dollars-and-sense" reasons that it's worth doing this right.

Between weekends, holidays, and summer breaks, school facilities are empty 50% of the year. It's tremendously wasteful from the taxpayers' standpoint. What can be done with those facilities?

Much greater brains than mine will need to begin to tackle this question, but it certainly is a community issue at large. Opening the buildings as they exist today to the community means a change in a community thinking process and a change in how schools not only are viewed, but how they operate. Remember, many school boards and superintendents are elected to their positions by the public; so public perception drives many of their decisions.

The fundamental concern of school boards has always been the taxpayer has already paid once for the building, so any use in the "off hours" should be for a small stipend or the cost of custodial care and maintenance. While there are some schools that open their doors to community events, for the most part, school administrators don't see any rewards or value in doing anything of scale and actually look on it as an intrusion into their space that causes stress over security and custodial issues.

Retrofitting already-existing buildings (at considerable cost) to provide the capacity for high-quality digital learning on a daily basis for thousands of students would have a tremendous side benefit: creating a massive community-owned asset that could potentially be used to entirely retrain the adult population of the United States without additional material expense!

But, of course, it probably won't be put to that use.

Why not? Because by the time the state or local school boards and the state, city, or county boards agree to work on a large-scale plan of action, the facilities will again be obsolete and the schools will go once again to the community for grants, to float bonds or to raise millage rates to start the cycle over. So once again we see the vast potential that could be squandered if we only reform *part* of the education process.

Beyond rethinking staffing, the physical plant, and the online spaces where so much learning will be taking place, we also need to reconsider the digital assets and consumables that will need to be managed and paid for. It's an absolutely vital consideration.

The idea of "no child left behind" may, in the coming years, truly become a nightmare, as the digital divide — access to digital curricula and assets leading to a major void between the haves and have-not — will find those who *have* far outpacing those who are left behind at an exponential rate.

The have-nots will fall behind at every level, from lacking the necessary skills to compete internationally, being unprepared for new required exams, and much, much more.

13   The most important job in today's school...

The role of the school site-based principal must change in a rapidly changing environment. While the majority of existing principals are going to need extensive retraining on how to incorporate effective and consistent models of blended learning, they are also going to need a deep knowledge of how to operate "school as a business model".

While the vast majority of principals do a great job of working within their assigned budgets, most of them lack any formal background in business or finance, and many recoil at the idea of their schools being a business. Remember, they entered the profession of education understanding it to be about the student, a service model. They have been trained to teach, to serve the children and families, to meet the needs of developing and coaching other professionals, and other such important tasks.

Some of the business that will come into question for the new school leader will come around the areas of virtual or blended learning support and management. The establishment of ongoing processes and the capacity to hire external contractors or part-time facilitators will become increasingly important. For the most part, these roles do not exist in the current school employee hierarchies.

Essentially, area number one will mean that the principal or district leader will have to have someone on staff that can customize the use of digital assets to meet their educational needs. This is much more difficult than selecting a textbook from an approved list. This will mean someone needs to be available to select online courseware, cloud-hosted platforms and services, web-based tools, online collaboration resources, tutoring resources, aggregated licensed content from multiple providers and publishers, evaluate online labs, and other instructional resources. And even if there's a budget to use to hire such an individual, the principal needs to be trained on how to recognize the best candidate for the job.

The new principal also needs to be able to market, to research and build processes for establishing the newly necessary relationships for the school in a digital age. They need to be able to offer private and public partnerships since they will be able to do everything they need to do on their school-site budget. Larger districts may be able to meet the needs for some of this, but in the smaller, independent school district (or in the private school) where there is limited additional staff, someone will need to be in charge of developing extensive dual-enrollment programs with more than the local community college, career and technical relationships for certification programs, all with an emphasis on quality for the academic integrity of the programs, and security to meet the needs of working with young students.

The principal will also need to have flexibility and capacity to recruit, screen, hire, and train part-time certified teachers to serve as adjuncts, facilitators, and graders for their school's digital programs. These individuals will need to understand existing audit-compliance paperwork in a new environment until such times as policies and processes come up to speed. It is only using the adjunct model that a transition period can be accomplished, but the union based employment models in many instances may preclude this from happening. Again, understanding the business model behind this is the only way the principal will be able to grow personalized education with blended-learning and virtual programs to sustainable numbers.

The way we communicate also changes in this new environment.

The school principal no longer needs to think about the monthly or weekly school newsletter, or the quarterly progress reports, (although there are still many schools with mandates in place for these to be produced in addition to the new communication tools being utilized, causing double the work.)

In this era of instant gratification and immediate access to information, parents, students, teachers, and all others with a direct interest in the school can (and will) request information, and expect to receive it in a timely manner.

The pressure on the principal will be to accurately and efficiently turn around information in a much faster, more detailed manner. To be honest, there are many principals, like teachers and support staff, who just won't find the job fulfilling when it loses its focus on helping children learn.

In this new era, the principal needs to be the one to guide the team in finding some kind of balance between this infusion of new technologies and controlling access as defined by existing policies, while simultaneously hoping to provide open access for effective teaching and learning. It is a delicate balance.

The role of the new principal is to advocate for the creation of a new set of standards that will enable the professionals working at that school site to deliver the optimum environment that supports personalized learning enhanced through the use of digital assets. And, in most cases, principals are on an annual contract without tenure, so there is absolutely no security for those hoping to be trailblazers if they rock the boat in their home environments.

Again, we must get to a point where we encourage and support school leadership in this new environment. It is undoubtedly the case where mistakes will be made, but we must create a climate where innovation is not stamped out before it even begins because school leaders are afraid to fail.

14 The most important job in today's school *system...*

Traditionally, the Chief Academic Officer, or assistant superintendent for curriculum, at the district- or school-level is the most academically minded member of the administration, someone with expertise in both content and standards.

In the pre-digital era world of education, the CAO's primary functions were oriented around textbook-adoption cycles, curriculum, and student testing and evaluation. But now that job model is turned upside-down.

The explosion of technology has fed the implosion of the textbook industry in a variety of ways, though the breakdown basically goes something like this:

First, students have a need for digital content, so e-readers replace textbooks. But kids get bored just as quickly with an e-reader as they did with regular texts. Attempts at app-based or piecemeal digital content place a huge burden on teachers to weave multiple pieces from different sources into one coherent curriculum.

Most teachers and schools are inadequately prepared to become content developers and curriculum writers while simultaneously teaching a full load of students, so *all* the jobs — new and old alike — suffer from the lack of attention. Schools then turn to external providers for curriculum cartridges or web/cloud-based courseware.

While some publishers offer great resources, inevitably a clash comes when school attempts at personalized learning intersects with inflexible cartridge content designed by the publisher.

District leadership has to be able to evaluate curricula by the new measures, but all they've learned in terms of textbook adoption is no longer relevant to a new paradigm... again, putting the new paradigm into the old box will not yield significant change.

The "common core" standards, devised by the states and content experts under the guidance of governors and state education chiefs, have been adopted by all but a handful of states (although ongoing debate may see some state governors drop out in the near future), but there are still concerns about how to apply those standards. Some of the heat in curriculum debate stems from question about the degree of granularity at issue.

Whether "curriculum" means a high-level outline or the fully developed content of a six-week science lesson dramatically affects the conversation, as teachers and administrators get more defensive of their "territory" the closer down the oversight comes.

Developing a curriculum for the modern school and its digitally enabled students is in many ways more involved and challenging than it was in the more traditional school system, though the core principles remain basically the same.

The International Association for K-12 Online Learning (iNACOL) sets out national standards for online courses on its website (www.inacol.org), providing an excellent starting point for building a framework for a digital class. Beyond that, an engaging design is more important than it was in the mimeographed lesson-plan era, but more crucial still is selecting appropriate content and incorporating resources currently available at the school site with all necessary copyright notices into engaging assignments for the digital classroom.

In an era where content becomes a commodity, and we are asking teachers to write and provide that commodity, there is still much work to be done around intellectual property rights, distribution rights in an online environment, and compensation for educators who are being asked to create, develop, enhance, or supplement curriculum in a new environment. It creates a whole set of legal ramifications for the district-level administrators in charge of curriculum and contracts.

No one wants to be the first "Napster of the school publishing industry" by being the case study district, charter organization, or private school brought to court because the teachers have all copied their textbooks, lessons and tests onto open-source learning management platforms thinking they had rights to do so just because they bought the book three years ago…..sorry teachers, that doesn't give you online distribution rights, and that's what you are doing by adding all those pdf's and videos into your free or open source online platforms.

When asked about digital content, some administrators will immediately talk about the need for an "adaptive" solution, identifying the sheer magnitude of the misunderstandings and lack of commonality in understanding terminology associated with this new modality. There is no consistent definition or understanding of the vocabulary of blended and virtual education.

One of the biggest concerns I have today is that schools and organizations are jumping quickly on the bandwagon of infusing technology into their classrooms, but are confusing the use of computer-based instruction models with what can really make a significant difference: when technology — and the data it can provide with regards to student learning — are implemented properly. The words "adaptive" and "predictive analytics" are bandied around by every vendor in the country, and we're beginning to see the misuse of this term showing up in educational jargon as part of a required set of standards for this new era.

They do not mean the same thing. There is not yet consistent use or understanding of the vocabulary of blended and virtual education models, despite the fact that iNacol and other high-quality organizations involved with instruction, design, quality assurance, and accreditation have clearly identified definitions. Loose interpretations mean that there is much confusion in the industry, even among those with experience.

Let's not confuse predictive analytics with computer-based instruction that provides responses to correct or incorrect answers and sends students down a pathway based upon those responses.

This form of computer-based instruction has been around for a decade or more and is absolutely not predictive analytics. One of the problems with this form of independent instruction using the computer is that many educators actually believe that this is helping the student by reinforcing the skill or concept, providing practice, and then helping the student move on to the next skill once he or she has "mastered" the prerequisite, or predetermined set of standards. In fact, there are a couple of problems associated with this "adaptive" solution.

First, kids have quickly learned to game the system, and so we've run into all kinds of academic integrity issues, whereby teachers have been involved in resetting the program until the student gets the right answer, not with any malicious intent, but simply because the fallacy has been perpetuated that, with enough practice, the student can go back and try that skill again until he demonstrates knowledge of the topic by passing.

Secondly, this type of computer-based instruction does not take into account very important factors about how the student is engaging with the content. For example, if Johnny is supposed to watch a video tutorial for five minutes before answering 10 questions, and the computer shows us that he actually only spent 30 seconds on the video, then he hasn't actually failed to demonstrate mastery of the content when he fails his 10 questions, all he's managed to demonstrate is laziness. In this case he should not be sent on a journey down the proverbial rabbit hole, with a whole new series of questions, he just needs somebody to "encourage" him to watch the video tutorial.

In addition, if Johnny receives his content in pictorial, video, or other visual format in addition to text, and we see that he responds well and works at a more rigorous level when he receives content in a format other than text, then we begin to notice patterns of behavior in how Johnny learns and can send him content based upon his learning style, as opposed to simply responding to incorrect answers.

Similarly, if Johnny learns a complex concept and demonstrates mastery of that concept by being able to analyze, synthesize, or produce new work as a result of his comprehension, but only does so with the benefits of a collaborative session either with the teacher or his peers, then we know that in order to truly raise the bar, we need to engage him (and other students like him) in learning that goes beyond computer-based instruction that simply responds to correct or incorrect answers.

Once we've sorted out our curriculum, we have to focus on individual learning.

In his book, <u>Beyond Technology: Questioning, Research and the Information Literate School Community</u> (F N O Pr, 2000), Jamie McKenzie explores key characteristics of scaffolding in the context of student learning experiences. defines "instructional scaffolding" as curriculum and instruction that hits six key benchmarks: clear direction that reduces students' confusion; clarifying purpose by helping students understand why they are doing the work and why it is important; keeping students on tasks by providing structure and clear pathways to learning; clarifying expectations and incorporating assessment and feedback using models of exemplary work, rubrics, and superior student work samples; pointing students to worthy sources that reduce confusion, frustration, and time, and offers them choices; and reducing uncertainty, surprise, and disappointment by offering multiple routes to success.

Providing students with the material, educational supports, and experiences that will help them master new competencies and skills will require systemic support from quarters that are currently far behind the curve in terms of understanding what's required. It will also demand new metrics to evaluate digital learners' progress.

Merging the best of what we know about the human brain, cognition, and learning, with where we know we need to go to take advantage of the technologies available to us today will undoubtedly result in new objectives for student learning, new ways of teaching, and, of course, new forms of student assessment. Today's technologies bring us great opportunities to provide every student with a virtual portfolio. This transportable sample of a student's best work, experiences, and practicum activities can include both written and multimedia formats.

Imagine students being able to deliver their work, and thereby their assessments, as a video project aligned to a rubric that is embedded in their virtual portfolio.

Imagine a student being able to document his community-service hours using pictures, video, and assessments placed in his portfolio via an invitation to share between his teacher and the person supervising the external activity.

These things are already happening in some of our schools at a time when some unfortunate children are still being subjected to dittos, multiple-choice questions, and rote memorization. I ask you, which form of assessment would you prefer your child participate in?

At a time when we are rewriting national exams, aligned to a national set of minimum standards embraced by many states, there is much outcry over whether or not the federal government should be interfering in what (or when) states choose to offer as the core or minimum curriculum.

The real outcry ought to be that we, as a nation, still have not accepted that a set of minimum standards is essential to evaluate progress in general, but we really should be looking at setting expectations much higher and pushing our brightest students to perform at a globally accelerated level.

If we continue to focus our attention on whether or not we even accept a set of common core standards, we are really missing the boat, and setting another generation up for mediocrity as the standard. It is long past time for a national education-reform task force to take the reins and offer suggestions with timelines and deliverables that can lead to the reform of our educational system. With all due respect to the federal government, they need to fund this research and then get out of its way.

They need to expect — and welcome — complete honesty from the researchers, not limit the scope of the research, so that it does not just give us what we need to hear to remain politically correct. We need to respect the findings in much the same way we would a cure for a disease by funding the solution as something in the best interests of the public health so that we can truly implement change.

And again with respect to my fellow educators who associate the research study with longitudinal data, this is not a ten-year study, because all the research is already available on the state of the union, and the focus should be placed upon analysis of existing data in order to focus on designing America's education for tomorrow. The best minds in education today, from both public and private enterprise, should be gathered into an innovation research and design center to work on this project.

While there are recognized experts that, of course, will be at the table, an interesting observation is how many of those educational reformers working to lead recent efforts to reform public education attended private schools themselves, suggesting that they know from experience what a less-bureaucratic, more student-focused approach can offer. But they cannot be the only guests at the table of reform. There needs to be that place for the absolutely unknown to contribute.

An invitation should be extended to the voices from the field who know best what is needed – because they are working in it every day – and give them an opportunity to interact with and engage in discussion with the brightest and sharpest technological minds who are working in the industry today. And no, this does not mean the CEOs of all the major companies, but much more likely to be the young guy in the back room who's writing the code who can translate the vision, the necessary functionality, and the processes into an actionable request for products, services and support systems. It needs to be a combination of people who understand the human brain, people who understand pedagogy in this modern age, people who understand the most advanced technologies we have today and who can therefore contribute to designing where the education industry will be before today's kindergarten students make their way through the school system.

They need to be paid appropriately for their work, for their travel, and for other expenses associated with this national priority. The federal government cannot be responsible for funding this, unless we want the reformers to be eating cereal for lunch and live in fear of running out of cellphone minutes when they're supposed to be sharing innovative and challenging experience. Okay, so I jest, but you get the point: this cannot be done properly on the government's budget without the sponsorship of major foundations, and I'm sure there are many out there more than willing to support a reform of our national education system. Can you imagine the systemic reform that could take place if these transformative opportunities were allowed to flourish?

With no paper trail, how do we monitor student progress and enable success?

15

Once we unleash the ability of students to make the most of tablets and other types of devices, we'll have come a long way towards remaking the educational system into one that serves the needs of the modern world.

Change will quickly prove meaningless unless it's coupled to a new approach to *what* we expect the students to learn, *how* we present it to them, and, most importantly, what we expect them to *do* with the information or content they have learned.

This means that we have to actually look at what we're teaching and define curriculum. Let's begin by agreeing that curriculum is not content. Essentially we have a set of standards, things that we believe students at a particular grade level can master, things we believe or have identified that they should know before moving on to the next grade level. To teach the content that's involved in demonstrating mastery of these standards at any given grade level, educators have outlined a scope and sequence of work that should address meeting these needs. Teachers have then selected textbooks as the source of content to help them teach to those standards.

For years, our education system has really allowed the textbook to be the source of the content we choose to teach at each grade level, and I choose at this point not to delve into variations within the industry. In this new digital age, wherein textbooks or e-readers are relegated to a position of being one of many resources available for teachers and students, we are now looking at what comprises good courseware, which curriculum works best for our students, and which of the many content pieces can be used to meet our needs on a daily basis in schools across the country.

For the first time we are moving away from a single textbook-based approach to a much newer content-aggregation approach in the educational system.

With so many options available today, the entire notion of a single source of information supplemented only by a dictionary or an encyclopedia is moot.

The digital solution is a learning-object-based approach to content that allows teacher access to a repository of millions of pieces of content tagged to multiple data points that can be sorted for students by many different criteria, among them subject area; standards; content type or format; activity level; level of rigor; and time on task.

Once we review the curriculum at this micro-level, we are able to begin truly personalizing education for every learner. Testing based on outdated standards doesn't necessarily provide the right direction and will repeat patterns that have already proven useless in the modern world. There are multiple factors to take into account: for instance, how does a given student learn from multiple media, tracked against time spent on multiple tasks, mapped against the anticipated time these tasks are estimated to take?

And of course, there's the notion of the Carnegie Unit, most simply defined as a single student, "Johnny," taking a single semester course to study "x" subject-area content, the completion of which will earn Johnny a half-semester "credit" towards graduation. This credit is usually earned over a period of time defined as 45 contact hours with an instructor. (Actual contact hours will, of course, vary depending upon the credit being awarded in the institution of record.)

Today's student, using technology, is no longer limited by time or space, and can therefore accelerate the learning process in ways never before utilized. Truth be told, the Carnegie Unit is no longer relevant in this new paradigm, and a new way of measuring to assess knowledge gained needs to be established as a commonly accepted standard so that students who can and do accelerate are not punished because they have not spent a prerequisite amount of time on the task at hand, defined by an archaic system of accountability.

What the new technologies provide is data-tracking capabilities to allow us to actually define a whole new process for measuring student performance. Imagine two students tackling content for standard "Y." Traditionally, if Johnny and Mary both pass with an "A" in the grade book, that does not take into account that while Johnny completed all of his assignments in one hour and did a much more in-depth project to present his findings, Mary took ten hours to complete the same work, and even though she answered each question and earned the points per the rubric the teacher had assigned, she had barely skimmed the surface of the topic and therefore had mastered at only a very superficial level.

Measuring levels of effort and engagement is key, and for determining how we transform education for the future, developing a metric for comparison between how students learn in independent learning versus "live" (or face-to-face, in-person) learning is critical.

The learning styles of the digital student are very different from those of their predecessors, and while good teachers can, as they always have, instruct them to pursue knowledge with more rigor and focus, there are specific areas that are very different from what has been expected of earlier, analog learners.

Bernie Trilling, the co-author of *21st Century Skills: Learning for Life in Our Times* (Jossey-Bass, 2009) and global director for the Oracle Education Foundation, describes the essential elements of today's student learning through a list of seven "C"s. He sees them in the following characteristics:

Critical thinking and problem solving
Creativity and innovation
Collaboration, teamwork, and leadership
Cross-culture understanding
Communication, information, and media literacy
Computing and ICT (Information and Communication Technology) literacy
Career and learning self-reliance

If we accept that Trilling's seven "C"s have a real validity as modern-day requisites of education, and if we can accurately gauge students' mastery and tie student promotion and eventual graduation to their level of accomplishment, we'll have achieved a real breakthrough in

95

preparing these students to join the modern workforce, giving them skills that will be better aligned to the "real world" than graduates have had in decades.

As a nation, we give much lip service to the notion of preparing students for the 21st-century workforce, but we do little to provide the quality of education students will need in order to engage in such a vision, and, to date, have done little to cultivate teachers who have the tools and training necessary to execute this vision.

16   Changing who (and what) is educating our nation's children...

The process by which we recruit and train educators for the new, digital-friendly schools we're envisioning is going to require at least as much transformation as the system by which we educate our children. As with every part of the reforms I've been discussing, we're going to have to transform the process by which we recruit and train new educators as well as the means by which we retrain those teachers who have the potential to hold teaching positions in the new educational order. And it's not just those who teach, we will also need to rethink everyone who works as a support to learners within the system.

Before we can train or recruit, we need to know what the new roles will be. What's needed is a new alignment, an understanding of the roles and functions of the new jobs that will be essential in a blended learning environment. It will not be as simple as simply handing out new job descriptions and presuming that teaching people how to use technology or tools will suffice. Once we understand the teaching and the learning process in a new paradigm, and we filter that perspective through the lens of "how does this affect student performance," we will be able to identify the new needs.

One likely change is that the technology guru who has generally led the way in the district or school for the last decade may be in a real quandary about getting the support necessary to lead this new strategic reform movement.

Ironically, the people within the school system who ought to be the most engaged champions for change are, in some cases, slow to embrace systemic reform. This is what we'll call the "Legacy Technology Guru."

Having risen to power because they have — or, really, *had* — the knowledge of technology as it pertained to mainframes, infrastructure, school reporting functions, and, in more recent times, school website development, these gatekeepers have stood in a hallowed spot because no one else knew *anything* about technology.

Today, some of these Chief Information Officers, CIOs or tech leaders, are incredibly reluctant to change, and not necessarily without cause. They have lived through technology implementations such as re-cabling entire districts to bring faster internet to the buildings; they have built labs with "champagne tastes, caviar dreams, and tap-water budgets" and were subjected to "lowest-bid technologies" even though they would never have recommended such products and services had they been able to get what they really wanted. They are also suffering from the "once bitten, twice shy" syndrome and know from more than a decade of experience that they are often asked to implement sweeping changes in technology without any kind of budget or staffing to support these grandiose ideas.

We've identified that we need to re-evaluate the physical space of the brick-and-mortar school, but we also need to re-examine who the people are that occupy

different roles in the education process as it relates to technology. The skill sets needed shift with every change in the tools and with changes in the implementation models. As a result, the old job descriptions may no longer apply, and the people that have held jobs with those titles may no longer be the appropriate people *for* those jobs, unless they have been meticulous about keeping up with the fast-changing pace of the tech world.

Just because someone had the knowledge and skill sets for technology even a decade ago does not mean that that same person is an essential contributor in operating educational technology environments today. This is one of those areas that cannot be defined by a degree in the subject area; rather the concept of "tech expertise" necessitates a new type of district technology leader, a shrewd strategic leader who can build or outsource an array of technical services based upon current projects and the needs of the district or school.

Most schools and districts are not set up to allow for technology leadership to have access to the budget and resources necessary to be able to contract services on an as-needed basis and with a fast turnaround time.

Most district-level technology leaders are tied to archaic budgeting paradigms that don't allow them to work in the same manner or with the same level of flexibility given to an equivalent corporate technology staff.

For the most part, the pain points here will be magnified at a time when support at the district level will be of ever-increasing importance, as support-staff teams on the technical side will have to be substantially bigger, either in the form of staff paid directly by the district or through sufficiently funded outsourcing of those jobs to third-party suppliers.

This will also be an area where payroll and budgeting will need to be revised. Most school districts or schools do not have a pay grade on their scales that would allow an entry-level or midrange programmer to have a beginning salary in the mid- to high $80,000s. In the school districts, where many superintendents earn salaries that top out around $150,000 per year, the idea of paying a top-end developer, or, worse yet, a team of such developers, the same salaries as the Superintendent would probably cause the head of finance to go into shock. But that's the reality of the skilled job market in educational technology today.

There is currently no such thing as federal or local support being given to a district with a direct line item to fund the kind of quality human capital they will need in this area, or to fund the ongoing extensive and essential training that needs to take place for full-time technology staff, and that needs to change immediately.

One thing is certain: the solution cannot just be giving everyone a piece of technology. Everyone having a tablet, laptop, or other device is only to get us so far, and if not implemented well, initiatives like this will compound existing problems, not solve them. Often these items are sold to schools on terms where students or the schools get to keep the technology after as long a period as four years. During that period, many such technologies will become obsolete several times over, so it's a bad deal all around, including for the site-based technology support staff that need to service these technologies or, at minimum, need to downgrade their use of time to become "packers and shippers" of technology to the source supplier.

Technology is a tool, not the answer to improving the education system, and it means nothing without the right people, processes, training and support behind the implementation.

Inroads are being made towards our goals of going digital in education. In 2000, there were some 80,000 online courses directed at K-12 students. In 2012, that number had ballooned to 4,000,000, so clearly digital media is going to find a place in the schools. In higher education, it is estimated that 20,000,000 online enrollments will take place in 2015. The question is, is our implementation going to be part of a haphazard patchwork — the way it currently stands in most school systems that have let it in over a period of the last ten to fifteen years — or as part of a unified approach that maximizes the potential of this constantly evolving platform.

As for smartphones and other "social" technologies in classrooms, the National Association of Secondary School Principals (NASSP) offers a position statement on their website, www.nassp.org, that characterizes mobile and social technologies as both crises and opportunities for leaders, saying confusion has, to date, led many school leaders to knee-jerk policy decisions, such as outright bans on specific technologies.

But these bans, in addition to being misguided, have been ineffective, making useful technologies far less productive and doing little to curb the bad behavior these bans were designed to deter. The NASSP identifies the guiding principles that frame their position and makes recommendations for school and district leaders. In addition, they emphasize that policymakers should also provide an appropriate funding stream, enact reasonable policies, and engage school leaders in conversations to inform those policies.

Instead of thinking of laptops and iPads or other tablets as passive devices used largely for note-taking or, more often, for entertainment and distraction, these devices should be seen as creating possibilities for mobile learning. The potential for mobile devices to deliver information to students' fingertips no matter where they are has many educators intrigued as an avenue that could help students take ownership of their education.

Teachers and administrators should think of tablets as being like a musical instrument. Without proper instruction, they are just noisy distractions, but when used properly, they can create things of beauty and value. The true power of tablets in the classroom comes when we teach students how to use them as instruments of blended learning, but this can only be accomplished if we are using those devices to deliver true digital content to students. The content has to be devised for this purpose, not retrofitted from a pre-digital world (no, scanning a textbook page and emailing the PDF isn't true digital content — it's also copyright infringement, but that's a different chapter).

Where the iPad/tablet experience can be most easily repurposed to educational endeavors is in displaying digital textbook content. Images can be rendered in three dimensions, visuals can be presented in remarkable fidelity, text can offer well-curated web links to areas of further study and, perhaps most amazingly, the can be updated as often as needed. No more waiting two years or more for a history text that recognizes who won the last Presidential election... or a science textbook that has to wait five years for the next cycle to correctly identify when Pluto is or is not a planet.

The trouble with classroom tablets is, as we've discussed earlier, that they are much more frequently used for passively receiving information or as a communication tool. There is nothing more wasteful than providing a student with an iPad and locking it down so that the student can only use it to receive e-mails, access calendars, or to communicate with the teacher. Doing creative work using technology is a higher-order activity that requires specific training for the teacher in different kinds of techniques and software use.

In February 2013, I had the pleasure of chairing a panel of experts for International Digital Learning Day in Puerto Rico. A 13-year-old eighth grader took the stage with Tom Vander Ark, author of *Getting Smart: How Digital Learning is Changing the World* (Jossey-Bass, 2011), and a half-dozen of his contemporaries, authors and distinguished K-12 educators who have led statewide public virtual schools, curriculum and technology companies, and international online programs.

The student took her place on stage and used her PowerPoint presentation with as much pizzazz as the adults. She answered the rapid-fire questions from members of the audience, and those that came in from the Internet. Her focus was simple, to encourage the adults on stage and those they represented in the educational space, to rethink education. She acknowledged that her eighth-grade teacher for language arts had given her a "B" that term, but that she really didn't care, because in her mind the work she was being asked to do was both trivial and irrelevant. She shared via live demonstration with the audience that she had an online following of thousands of other young people, that she wrote multiple times each day, that she often invited guest authors into her online world to share thoughts with her followers, that she had a set of standards and monitored for appropriate language and ideas, edited and researched for her audience, and much more.

How ironic that the traditional middle school classroom was not capable of capturing this passion, and that the teacher was not able to share an online world wherein the "B" student was actually engaging in all the complex thought processes of researching, synthesizing, creating, demonstrating, and producing work that we would like our university-level students to engage in.

A number of studies have found that social networks and other online groups open up whole new worlds of learning that schools have, up until now, failed to explore, and that time spent online is highly important for teenage development. It is essential for those developing policies around social media in the classroom to consider all aspects, and not to reduce the potential of online interaction due to fear of a small number of students engaging in inappropriate behavior.

There is an entire subculture of online activity, networking, and authentic experiences that is creating another whole dimension for digital learners; and understanding how these learners rely on their technology is a necessary component to educating them.

According to "The Truth About Youth," a report on the findings of a 2011 study conducted by McCann Worldgroup, more than half of those studied said that they "would rather give up their sense of smell than their technology."

Depriving students in school of unfettered use of the information-based technology they use everywhere else in their lives is another way the educational system makes school a place that seems utterly irrelevant to today's young people. The McCann report finds that the two biggest impediments that students say they face as far as their technology usage are filters that stop them from accessing the websites they need for homework, and bans on using their own mobile devices (namely cellphones) at school.

This sort of awareness of how the digital generation is different from any that came before it is crucial to the success of any sweeping, systemic reform.

17 There's no time like the... actually, there's no time

One thought that must remain front-of-mind as we contemplate the design our new educational system will follow, is that education, at its core, is a *service business*. So what we need, ultimately, is a better *service model*.

The great thing about the competitive market of ideas in education that we've been discussing here is that, in it, we can put bold initiatives against one another and the one that delivers the best results for students will win. The key is being as open to many ideas, and having no fear about trying new things.

Similarly, regardless of whatever path to reform we take, we can't embrace big, sweeping changes only to ultimately declare, "Okay, we've caught up" and rest on our laurels. As the technology that our digital learners live with from birth continues to evolve, a constant cycle of revisions and customizations will be necessary on our end just to keep up.

It's important for administrators to keep this in mind as they consider vendors and technologies that will be part of the move towards systemic reform. Pretty websites with flashy design are nice, but what do they really deliver? The steak, not the sizzle, is what matters (apologies to my vegetarian friends for the analogy).

106

Similarly, it doesn't need to be the most expensive option. **As is evidenced over and over again, there is no correlation between costs and results. However, there is no doubt in my mind that there is a direct correlation between results and the level of commitment.**

There is great potential throughout the education system. Despite the bad rap teachers get, the vast majority of them are dedicated professionals who want to engage their students and help them learn. Unfortunately, the system removes any incentive to experiment and try new things to keep up with a student population that, like every generation before it, thinks it has all the answers. The difference, as we've seen, is that, thanks to modern technology, this generation really *does* have easy access to the answers.

To unlock this potential on the teaching side, we must be supportive to teachers who encourage and inspire students to do great work.

If we want students to produce great work, we have to stop preventing them from using the tools, which means we have to review any policy that restricts the use of those tools, from restricting web access to disabling tablets' cameras.

Today's students are collaborative, flexible, and discerning in their approach to the world of knowledge that's at their fingertips, and we need to craft an educational system that reflects and encourages the best aspects of that reality. The purpose of today's schools, and the environment we need to create, is one that is creative, critical, and provides opportunities for self-analysis and review so that students can change tracks as needed.

107

Human growth and development is the most complex issue any organization deals with and that is the entirety of what education is about. By changing the way the learning ecosystem functions, moving kids ahead based on personal mastery of skills rather than simply by recitation of facts and seniority, we will redefine the future of learning. That future is the future of our children... giving students the opportunity to make choices now will teach them to be flexible, better preparing them for the grown-up world they'll graduate into.

Already, the average American changes careers seven times in their lifetime and the Department of Labor's most recent statistics suggest that the future belongs to the entrepreneurial class.

In success, we can strengthen the American family, as greater flexibility of schooling can better enable a parent to participate in their child's education. We can strengthen the intellect, values, and general work ethic of young adults, creating a workforce that can compete for the jobs of today... and tomorrow.

18 The revolution starts with you!

At the beginning of this book, I talked about the idea of the American educational system having gone past the metaphorical crossroads many many times, at each intersection choosing paths that offered, at best, superficial changes. And the consequences of taking the easy path grow more obvious, and more devastating, every day.

Maintaining failing structures — both ideological and physical — and tinkering with existing systems won't generate the results that are necessary to completely reform schools to serve their proper function: teaching students how to think critically and navigate the increasingly complex, integrated world of technology and achievement. We need to build a new system from the ground up.

Activism on the part of politicians, school administrators, teachers, students, and parents, are all an absolute necessity to build a new vision and a new educational reality. Our website, www.SystemicReform.com, is a place where you can share stories of your successes to inspire others, and your setbacks (they're inevitable in any reform initiative) to see if members of our community can offer ways to help. We're all in this together.

Innovation and transformation are risky, even terrifying, concepts, but not more terrifying than what

happens to the 56 million students in the U.S. whose futures depend on us if we don't do something *today*.

They can't wait, and neither can we.

We must dream big.

APPENDIX A: A TIMELINE OF AMERICAN PUBLIC EDUCATION 1635-PRESENT

While by no means a complete survey of all the twists and turns public education has taken since the 17th century, I've attempted to condense some of the most important changes to the system. Beyond the court cases that have changed school admission policies and what services must be provided, we can see when such change-bringing technologies as ballpoint pens, whiteboards, and personal computers became part of student life and recognize that these were all deeply disruptive at the time and the world did not come to an end.

The following is freely adapted and excerpted from the Applied Research Center website: http://www.arc.org/content/view/100/217/ and from American Educational History: A Hypertext Timeline: http://www.eds-resources.com/educationhistorytimeline.html.

1635
The first "free school" in Virginia opens.

1647
The General Court of the Massachusetts Bay Colony decrees that every town of fifty families or more should have an elementary school and that every town of 100 families or more should have a Latin school.

1779

Thomas Jefferson proposes a two-track educational system, with different tracks, in his words, for "the laboring and the learned".

1785

The Continental Congress (before the U.S. Constitution was ratified) passes a law calling for a survey of the Northwest Territory which created "townships," reserving a portion of each township for a local school. From these "land grants" eventually came the U.S. system of "land grant universities," the public state universities that exist today.

1790

The Pennsylvania state constitution calls for free public education but only for poor children. It is expected that rich people will pay for their own children's schooling.

1801

James Pillans invents the blackboard.

1805

The New York Public School Society is formed by wealthy businessmen to provide education for poor children. Schools are run on the "Lancasterian" model, in which one "master" can teach hundreds of students in a single room. The master gives a rote lesson to the older students, who then pass it down to the younger students.

1817

A petition presented in the Boston Town Meeting calls for establishing of a system of free public primary schools.

1820s

The first public high school in the U.S., Boston English, opens.

1827

Massachusetts passes a law making all grades of public school open to all pupils free of charge. In addition, Massachusetts towns of more than 500 families are required to have a public high school open to all students.

1837

Horace Mann becomes head of the newly formed Massachusetts State Board of Education.

1837

Louisville, Kentucky, appoints the first school superintendent.

1840s

Over a million Irish immigrants arrive in the United States, driven out of their homes in Ireland by the potato famine. Irish Catholics in New York City struggle for local neighborhood control of schools as a way of preventing their children from being force-fed a Protestant curriculum.

1848

Massachusetts Reform School at Westboro, where children who have refused to attend public schools are sent, opens.

This begins a long tradition of "reform schools," which combine the education and juvenile justice systems.

1851-1918
The State of Massachusetts enacts the first compulsory education law. By 1885, sixteen states have compulsory-attendance laws, but most of those laws are sporadically enforced at best. All states have them by 1918, helping to eliminate child labor in the United States.

1856
The first kindergarten in the U.S. opens in Watertown, Wisconsin. Four years later, the first "formal" kindergarten is established in Boston, Massachusetts.

1857
The National Teachers Association (now the National Education Association) is founded by forty-three educators in Philadelphia.

1862
The "Land Grant Act" becomes law. It donates public lands to states, the sale of which will be used for the "endowment, support, and maintenance of at least one college where the leading object shall be... to teach such branches of learning as are related to agriculture and the mechanic arts, in order to promote the liberal and practical education of the industrial classes in the several pursuits and professions in life." Many prominent state universities can trace their roots to this legislation and its subsequent expansion in 1890.

1865-1877
African-Americans mobilize to bring public education to the South for the first time. With the legal end of slavery, African-Americans in the South make alliances with white Republicans to push for many political changes, including, for the first time, rewriting state constitutions to guarantee free public education.

1867
The U.S. Department of Education is created in order to help states establish effective school systems.

1869
Boston creates the first public day school for the deaf.

1874
The Michigan State Supreme Court rules that Kalamazoo may levy taxes to support a public high school, setting an important precedent for similar rulings in other states.

1884
The first practical fountain pen is patented by Lewis Waterman.

1892
Formed by the National Education Association to establish a standard secondary school curriculum, the "Committee of Ten" recommends a college-oriented high school curriculum.

1893-1913
Size of school boards in the country's 28 biggest cities is cut

in half. Most district- or ward-based positions are eliminated in favor of citywide elections.

1901

Joliet Junior College, in Joliet, Illinois, opens. It is the first public community college in the U.S.

1905

The U.S. Supreme Court requires California to extend public education to the children of Chinese immigrants.

1906

The Carnegie Foundation for the Advancement of Teaching is chartered by an act of Congress. The Foundation encourages the adoption of a standard system for equating "seat time" (the amount of time spent in a class) to high school credits. Still in use today, this system came to be called the "Carnegie Unit".

1917

The Smith-Hughes Act passes, providing federal funding for vocational education. (It remains in force until its repeal in 1997).

1919

The Progressive Education Association is founded with the goal of reforming American education; by this time all states have laws providing funds for transporting children to school.

1926

The Scholastic Aptitude Test (SAT), based on the Army Alpha test, is first administered.

1931

Alvarez vs. the Board of Trustees of the Lemon Grove (California) School District becomes the first successful school desegregation court case in the United States, as the local court forbids the school district from placing Mexican-American children in a separate "Americanization" school.

1938

Ladislas Biro and his brother Georg patent the ballpoint pen.

1939

A national conference on student transportation results in the adoption of standards for the nation's school buses, including the shade of yellow.

1945

At the end of World War II, the G.I. Bill of Rights gives thousands of working-class men college scholarships for the first time in U.S. history.

1946

In *Mendez vs. Westminster and the California Board of Education*, the U. S. District Court in Los Angeles rules that educating children of Mexican descent in separate facilities is unconstitutional; Congress approves the National School Lunch Act.

1947

The Truman Commission Report recommends sweeping changes in higher education, including doubling college enrollments by 1960 and extending free public education through the establishment of a network of community colleges which would, in the 1960s, see community-college enrollment more than triple.

1948

In the case of McCollum v. Board of Education, the Supreme Court rules that schools cannot allow "released time," which allows students to participate in religious education in their public school classrooms, during the school day; Educational Testing Service is formed, merging the College Entrance Examination Board, the Cooperative Test Service, the Graduate Records Office, the National Committee on Teachers Examinations and others, with huge grants from the Rockefeller and Carnegie foundations.

1954

In *Brown v. Board of Education of Topeka*, the U.S. Supreme Court unanimously agrees that segregated schools are "inherently unequal" and must be abolished.

1957

A federal court orders integration of Little Rock, Arkansas public schools. Governor Orval Faubus sends his National Guard to physically prevent nine African American students from enrolling at all-white Central High School. President Eisenhower sends federal troops to enforce the court order.

1959

The ACT Test is first administered.

1963
In response to the large number of Cuban immigrant children arriving in Miami after the Cuban Revolution, Coral Way Elementary School starts the "nation's first bilingual public school in the modern era".

1965
The Elementary and Secondary Education Act (ESEA) is passed, providing federal funds to help low-income students, which results in the initiation of educational programs such as Title I and bilingual education; the Higher Education Act increases federal aid to higher education and provides for scholarships, student loans, and establishes the National Teachers Corps; Project Head Start, a preschool education program for children from low-income families, begins as an eight-week summer program.

1968
The Bilingual Education Act, also known as Title VII, becomes law (the law is repealed in 2002 and replaced by the No Child Left Behind Act); McCarver Elementary School in Tacoma, Washington becomes the nation's first magnet school.

1969
Herbert R. Kohl's book, *The Open Classroom,* helps to promote open education, an approach emphasizing student-centered classrooms and active, holistic learning.

1971

Michael Hart, founder of Project Guttenberg, invents the e-Book.

1972

Texas Instruments introduces the first in its line of electronic hand-held calculators; Title IX of the Education Amendments of 1972 becomes law, prohibiting discrimination based on sex in all aspects of education.

1974

In *Milliken v. Bradley*, the U.S. Supreme Court rules that schools may not be desegregated across school districts; in *Lau v. Nichols*, the Court rules that school districts must provide equal opportunities for all students, including those who do not speak English; Federal Judge Arthur Garrity orders busing of African American students to predominantly white schools in order to achieve racial integration of public schools in Boston, MA.

1975

The Education of All Handicapped Children Act becomes federal law. States are given until 1978 (later extended to 1981) to fully implement the law.

1977

Apple Computer, now Apple Inc., introduces the Apple II, one of the first successful personal computers. IBM follows suit with its PC, the model 5150, in 1981.

1980s

The federal Tribal Colleges Act establishes a community

college on every Indian reservation, which allows young people to go to college without leaving their families.

1981

John Holt's book, *Teach Your Own: A Hopeful Path for Education,* adds momentum to the homeschooling movement.

1982

Madeline C. Hunter's book, *Mastery Teaching,* is published. Her direct-instruction teaching model becomes widely used as teachers throughout the country attend her workshops and become "Hunterized".

1983

The report of the National Commission on Excellence in Education, *A Nation at Risk,* calls for sweeping reforms in public education and teacher training. Among its recommendations is a call for expanding high school requirements to include the study of computer science.

1985

In *Wallace v. Jaffree,* the U.S. Supreme Court finds that Alabama statutes authorizing silent prayer and teacher-led voluntary prayer in public schools violate the First Amendment.

1990

The Milwaukee Parental Choice program is initiated, allowing "students, under specific circumstances, to attend at no charge, private sectarian and nonsectarian schools located in the city of Milwaukee"; Teach for America is formed, reestablishing the idea of a National Teachers Corps.

1991

Minnesota passes the first "charter school" law; the smart board (interactive white board) is introduced by SMART Technologies.

1992

City Academy High School, the nation's first charter school, opens in St. Paul, Minnesota.

1993

The Massachusetts Education Reform Act requires a common curriculum and statewide tests (Massachusetts Comprehensive Assessment System). Other states follow Massachusetts' lead and implement similar high-stakes testing programs; Jones International University becomes the first university "to exist completely online".

1994

The Improving America's Schools Act (IASA) is signed into law by President Bill Clinton on January 25th. It includes reforms for Title I; increased funding for bilingual and immigrant education; and provisions for public charter schools, drop-out prevention, and educational technology.

1994

Proposition 187 passes in California, making it illegal for children of undocumented immigrants to attend public school. Federal courts hold Proposition 187 unconstitutional;

CompuHigh, which claims to be the first online high school, is founded.

1994-1995
Whiteboards find their way into U.S. classrooms in increasing numbers and begin to replace the blackboard.

1995
Georgia becomes the first state to offer universal preschool to all four year olds whose parents choose to enroll them.

1998
The Higher Education Act is amended and reauthorized requiring institutions and states to produce "report cards" about teacher education.

2001
The No Child Left Behind Act (NCLB) is approved by Congress and signed into law by President George W. Bush on January 8, 2002. The law mandates high-stakes student testing, holds schools accountable for student achievement levels, and provides penalties for schools that do not make adequate yearly progress.

2002
In *Zelman v. Simmons-Harris*, the U.S. Supreme Court rules that certain school voucher programs are constitutional and do not violate the Establishment Clause of the First Amendment.

2003

The North American Council for Online Learning (NACOL), a non-profit organization dedicated to enhancing K-12 online education, is "launched as a formal corporate entity".

2007

In the cases of *Parents involved in Community Schools v. Seattle School District No. 1* and *Meredith v. Jefferson County Board of Education*, the U.S. Supreme Court rules that race cannot be a factor in assigning students to high schools.

2009

The American Reinvestment and Recovery Act of 2009 provides more than ninety billion dollars for education, nearly half of which goes to local school districts to prevent layoffs and for school modernization and repair and includes the Race to the Top initiative, a 4.35-billion-dollar program designed to induce reform in K-12 education; the Common Core State Standards Initiative, "a state-led effort coordinated by the National Governors Association Center for Best Practices (NGA Center) and the Council of Chief State School Officers" is launched.

2010

With the U.S. economy mired in a recession and unemployment remaining high, states have massive budget deficits. As many as 300,000 teachers face layoffs, with thousands more announced in the years that follow.

2011

In spite of workers' protests and Democratic legislators leaving the state to delay the vote, the Wisconsin legislature passes a bill removing most collective-bargaining rights from many public employees, including teachers.

2013

On January 11, the *Washington Post* reports that Seattle high school teachers have refused to give the district-mandated Measures of Academy Progress exams, joining a "growing grass-roots revolt against the excessive use of standardized tests."; the Chicago Board of Education votes to close 50 schools, the largest mass closing in U.S. history.

Recommended Reading:

Getting Smart: How Digital Learning is Changing the World
Tom Vander Ark

Disrupting Class
Clayton Christensen, Michael Horn and Curtis Johnson

www.iNACOL.org
iNACOL STANDARDS FOR QUALITY ONLINE LEARNING

iNACOL STANDARDS FOR QUALITY ONLINE TEACHING

iNACOL STANDARDS FOR QUALITY ONLINE PROGRAMS

iNACOL's New Learning Models Vision: Keeping Pace with K-12 Online and Blended Learning

Online and Blended Learning: A Survey of Policy and Practice from K-12 Schools around the World
> Michael K. Barbour, Regina Brown, Lisa Hasler Waters, Rebecca Hoey, Jeffrey Hunt, Kathryn Kennedy, Chantal Ounsworth, Allison Powell, Trina Trimm, November 2011

www.ingramcontent.com/pod-product-compliance
Lightning Source LLC
LaVergne TN
LVHW011244080426
835509LV00005B/620